The Chinese Chicken Cookbook

More Than 100 Easy-to-Prepare,
Authentic Recipes for
the American Table

Eileen Yin-Fei Lo

Calligraphy by San Yan Wong

Simon & Schuster
New York   London   Toronto   Sydney   Singapore

SIMON & SCHUSTER
Rockefeller Center
1230 Avenue of the Americas
New York, NY 10020

Designed by Jaime Putorti

Manufactured in the United States of America

10   9   8   7   6   5   4   3   2   1

Library of Congress Cataloging-in-Publication Data
Lo, Eileen Yin-Fei.
The Chinese chicken cookbook : more than 100 easy-to-prepare, authentic recipes for the
American table / Eileen Yin-Fei Lo ; calligraphy by San Yan Wong.
p. cm.
Inclues index.
ISBN 978-1-4767-3207-7
1. Cookery (Chicken) 2. Cookery, Chinese. I. Title.

TX 750.5.C45L624 2004
641.6'65--dc22
2003059042

For information regarding special discounts for bulk purchases,
please contact Simon & Schuster Special Sales at 1-800-456-6798
or business@simonandschuster.com

This book, as always, is dedicated to my family. To my husband, Fred, tireless researcher, taster, and tyrant. To my daughter, Elena, and son Christopher, whose love of food and cooking approaches my own. To my son Stephen, the family's extraordinary eater. Finally, this book belongs as much to my agent, Carla Glasser, as to me; she makes me write, write.

Contents

The
Chinese Chicken
Cookbook

中國鷄菜食譜

Chicken at the Chinese Table

MYTHOLOGY OF THE PHOENIX

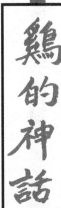

*I*t is believed among the Chinese that many foods are symbolic and are actually metaphors for aspects of life. In Chinese religions, folklore, allegory, and mythology, particular foods often have meanings and significance beyond satisfying hunger. Chicken, historically, is such a food.

To the Chinese the chicken is the embodiment of the phoenix, the mythological bird that rose from its ashes, symbolizing rebirth and reaffirmation. It is also a female symbol and is paired with the dragon, the male symbol, as a recurring image of marriage. Chicken is also believed to be a food that promotes longevity as well as a tonic that possesses recuperative powers (a concept shared with a number of cultures around the world).

As such it is part of every Lunar New Year celebration, every wedding feast, every birth of a child, every birthday and anniversary dinner in China. Chickens are offered whole to ancestors in temples and at graves. The whole chicken suggests that the lives of those departed were felicitous from beginning to end.

The chicken has always been a most honored food in China. It is highly regarded for its eggs, later its meat, still later for the life and flavor it provides for stocks and broths when it becomes too old to produce eggs and too tough to eat. The Chinese even distinguish between a chicken, an old hen, and an old and tough black-boned chicken. Each provides flavor for soup as well as nourishment, but the old hen is deemed better than the chicken, the black-boned chicken

better than the old hen. In all of its varieties it is a most useful, necessary, and esteemed bird, one that began its existence as a wild bird and was first domesticated in China thousands of years ago.

The whole chicken is a most versatile ingredient in the Chinese kitchen. The chicken is steamed, boiled, baked, stir-fried, deep-fried, braised, roasted, and barbecued. It is chopped, sliced, ground, and minced and cooked with rice and noodles. Often, in classic and traditional dishes, chicken is cooked using several processes for a single dish. Chicken is the basis for stocks and sauces and is often cooked with other ingredients. It is eaten hot or cold or at temperatures in between, in salads and in stews. Chicken fills baked and steamed buns and breads, is wrapped into dim sum dumplings and pastries, and is the inspiration for sculpted dough dumplings. No part of a chicken is wasted, from the meat and bones to the skin, the fat and the innards, and even the feet, which are a delicacy in China.

It is rare in China to come upon a region, a city, a town or village that does not have its own way of preparing chicken. Indeed, if you ask the chef in any restaurant how chicken is cooked in a particular area, you will be told that it is cooked "our way." In Beijing, chicken might be cooked in strips with sautéed leeks; in Guangzhou, simmered in soy sauce or roasted to a parchment-like crispness; in Hunan, cooked with chilies and bits of dried tangerine skin. In South China, chicken is often combined with the local tropical fruits; in Shanghai, it might be sweet and oily, or "drunken" with a marinade of rice wine; in Fujian, chicken is cooked together with rice. In dim sum teahouses it is stuffed into steamed dumplings or even into cakes of bean curd. Chicken might be sliced and ladled into rice congees, and in Hangzhou chicken could come wrapped in clay or pastry in a well-known dish called beggar's chicken. The number of chicken recipes is truly infinite.

Chickens, along with pigs, are believed to be the first wild animals to be domesticated. In their wild states, both animals were important foods for the P'ei-li-kaang, a prehistoric people who lived in what is now the central valley of the Yangzi River.

The chicken is mentioned as a domesticated bird in the oracle bone writings of the Shang/Yin dynasty, which spanned the period from 1766 to 1122 B.C., and chicken bones have been found in archaeological excavations of that period. It is believed that the chicken became a largely domesticated bird in those Shang years.

Excavations of Han dynasty tombs in Hunan in the last century have yielded much knowledge of the early Chinese kitchen and its foods. In one uncovered tomb, the preserved body of a woman, thought to be the wife of a nobleman, was found along with forty-eight bamboo boxes that have provided food historians with extensive information on Chinese eating and drinking in that 200 B.C. period. More than fifty pottery containers filled with various foods, including chicken, were found in that tomb as well. There were remains and writings about what were initially called "bamboo chickens," later "black chickens," terms for wild chickens, as well as notes on their domestication.

In another Han dynasty tomb, there are wall drawings of two chickens. In still another there is a detailed wall drawing of a kitchen scene that includes a rack on which hang two chickens.

Among the Han, an important feast always included a chicken dish. At the same time the Han rulers urged rural people to raise chickens, thus making them more accessible and no longer a food available only to nobility. The Han, according to the classic study *Food in Chinese Culture* (1981, Yale University Press), always offered chicken to honored guests, a custom so widespread that when it did not occur it was considered notable. Thus, one Han-period writer excuses a wealthy man for not providing chicken to his guests because it was needed to nourish the man's aged mother. Another tale is of an old woman, poor and ill, who steals a neighbor's chicken to cook a nourishing soup for herself and for a presumably ill daughter-in-law.

Through the years of China's various dynasties, particularly the Ming, from A.D. 1368 to 1644, mentions of chicken abound, always with admonitions that they be live and fresh. The Ming, notorious for gastronomic excess, appear to have regarded chickens as special indeed. More than six thousand cooks labored in the Ming imperial kitchens, a number that grew to nine thousand by the middle of the fifteenth century. Among them was a group whose function was to prepare foods for sacrifice to the heavens. Each year this group sacrificed 200,000 animals of which 138,000 were chickens.

Scholars on the subject of food and wine in China's long history were explicit and precise in their writings about chicken. In the Qing dynasty, China's last, which stretched from 1644 to 1912, scholar Yuan Mei wrote a book called *Shih-Tan*, which stressed the properties of food and the necessity for them to be cooked in such a manner as to balance the systems of those who ate them. He stressed that a chicken must not be eaten too young or too old, but in its prime and that it had to be cooked at precisely the right heat. Another Qing writer, Li Yu, was more philosophical. He valued chickens highly, he said, because they woke humans each day. Still another writer, Shen Fu, wrote warmly of a special "chicken soup with skin" cooked by his wife, Yuen. What is significant, to be sure, is that chicken was deemed sufficiently important to write about.

A banquet menu from the 1754 imperial court of Qian Long consisted of many small dishes, such as snacks, breads, and sweets. The seven main courses all contained chicken: a dish of fat chicken and bean curd; pot-boiled chicken, smoked fat chicken, and court-style fried chicken were a few of the dishes served.

Historically in many parts of China, chickens were eaten only occasionally because the chicken was considered too valuable as a source for its eggs to be killed and eaten for a single meal. Careful note was made of a chicken's age; thus when they became too old—both hens and roosters—they were killed for the richness they added to broths and stocks. To this day it is believed, as a matter of course, that old chickens make the best soups. It is true; they do.

Chickens were quite special in my family when I was growing up in the village of Siu Lo Chen, or "Lo's Little Village," in Sun Tak (today it is Shunde), a suburb of Guangzhou. Our family had its own chickens, which we raised from chicks. We would buy chicks, dye their feathers to indicate our ownership and then allow them to run free and to forage. We did not know the term "organic" or "free range," but that is indeed what they were. And even as they grew and we continued to tint their feathers, we would know our chickens and they would know us.

After the chickens ran free all day we would collect them by strewing small amounts of rice kernels while softly calling, "chiu, chiu, chiu." The chickens would come toward us and we would continue saying, *lai, lai, lai,"* or "come, come, come." Along with the raw rice, we would show them bowls of milled rice husks moistened with water from washed rice. They would run after us, right to their cages, which we would drape with black cloths so that they would rest at night. Each morning, we would free them again.

Our family valued the eggs from our chickens and we ate them in a variety of ways. We boiled them; cooked them in a sweet and pungent soy sauce–based *lo soi* liquid; and stewed them in sweet and savory custards. A special concoction called sweet birth vinegar, in which eggs were boiled and combined with strong rice vinegar, chunks of ginger, and pig's knuckles, was traditionally fed to women who had just given birth to build up their blood. It is a custom I followed with the births of each of my three children.

We believed that the chicken that gave the egg also conferred health and balance within one's body and helped in the recovery from illnesses. Chicken implicitly was good to us and for us. On its own it is considered a warming food. When combined in soup with cooling vegetables, it will become cooling. When strong herbs are added it will become a warming soup. Cooling soups are believed by practitioners of Chinese medicine to be ideal for reducing the body's temperature; carefully made "neutral" soups are considered perfect for the young as nourishment; warming soups benefit the elderly who fatigue easily, or those whose blood might be sluggish.

Herbalists often prescribe chicken broths with their prescriptions as beneficial, natural combinations. They believe chicken affects the stomach, liver, and spleen, and tones blood. Chicken and its soup warm the essential center of one's body and are prescribed often for appetite loss, weakness, loss of weight, diabetes, rheumatic pain, and blurred vision. One of my aunts, Ng Gu Jieh, had a keen knowledge of herbal medicine. Our family would often seek her advice as to which herbs and roots should be added to our soups to help us recover from illnesses. As a young girl I remember our family asking exactly what we should add to our chicken soup.

The chickens we enjoyed were roasted or barbecued, but we ate them steamed and stir-fried, as well as in soups and congees. As in virtually all other Chinese families, chicken was part of our blending of the sacred and the secular.

Our family always ate chicken on special occasions. We observed birthdays, engagements, and weddings with chicken. Before the wedding ceremony, the families of the bride and groom would come together to eat congees with chicken, for its symbolism. Chicken, a symbol of rebirth, was an important part of the dinners we ate on the eve of the Lunar New Year and on the second day of the New Year when we would cook and serve a chicken to note *hoi lin,* or the "opening of the year." At the traditional feast given to honor a baby one month after its birth, chicken dishes were always served.

Food offerings always indicated the importance of occasions; the more significant the occasion, the grander the offering. We believed in the dictum of Confucius, who wrote that a good man, "though his food might be coarse rice and vegetable soup, would offer a little of it in sacrifice with a grave, respectful air." Our family offerings included chickens in a tradition and observance overseen by my grandmother Ah Paw (Chinese for "mother's mother"). We would set out whole cooked chickens before our family ancestral altar at home and in the temples we visited.

We would take our offerings of food to the temple and there light incense sticks and candles. We would kneel, pray to the gods, offer them our food, particularly those whole chickens, so that they would give us their blessings for a good harvest and for good business. It was also considered a grateful gesture to the gods, a *wan sun,* to thank them for caring for those departed members of our family. Then we would take the chickens home, poach them in stock, and cut them up to eat as white cut chicken, our way of personally sharing in the ancestral offering.

We also offered chickens at the graves of our ancestors during the Ching Ming festival, celebrated each spring with a visit to these graves and a general tidying up of the gravesites.

Even in modern China having chickens, and of course their eggs, was a characteristic of those who were well off. The eldest son of a family was privileged to eat two eggs at breakfast, and after a woman had given birth she was served one poached egg per day, and chicken and soup from chicken at all her other meals, bounties not necessarily shared by other family members. After a birth, the family of the new mother would send out gifts of chickens and eggs, and distributing red-dyed boiled eggs was akin to the western tradition of handing out cigars.

It was believed in parts of southern China that cock's blood kept bad spirits at bay, and among the Fujian people—those who sailed to and settled in Southeast Asia—chicken blood, dried and fashioned into a loaf, was sliced and served with a variety of sauces.

Chickens in China were always live, always free running, always freshly killed. We never had such items as chicken "parts," which are commonplace in today's markets, though we often used portions of our chickens (legs, wings, breasts) for different preparations. We killed chickens, prepared them, and cooked and ate the whole thing. Occasionally we bought them, but always live ones. Even in a teeming city like today's Hong Kong, chickens are sold fresh and live in its central market. Housewives still shop twice each day for the noon meal and for dinner. When Ah Paw sent her servants out to buy chickens she would always wag her fingers at them, cautioning them to make certain the bird they bought was *"sun sin, sun sin,"* or "fresh, fresh," and should be *"fei, fei"* or big-breasted and meaty.

Every year on Ah Paw's birthday her cooks would prepare raw fish dishes for her, along with a whole chicken simmered in soy sauce, in her honor. The raw fish were deemed to be too strong for young stomachs, so as a child I was not permitted to eat them. Instead Ah Paw would have a thick, rich, rice congee filled with chicken made for me and my young cousins, something I always looked forward to at her birthday dinners, along with her chicken in soy sauce, which I was permitted to eat.

There is a recipe in this book for Ah Paw's chicken congee, of course, and for her soy sauce chicken, but you will find more than one hundred preparations for chicken from all over China, as well. All of the recipes are Chinese—traditional, classic, and modern. Many of them are my personal adaptations of classics. Some of these traditions cannot be broken but some can be altered slightly to fit the modern kitchen and I have done that. Along with these recipes are some personal notes and observations, some of my experiences, some bits of history, tradition, folk tales, and mythology as they relate to chicken.

An important note: much is made these days about cooking with wine. Most of the recipes in this book call for the addition of wine, particularly Shao-Hsing rice wine, in marinades, sauces, and in the actual cooking. This is not unusual. A caution: Do not use rice wine labeled "cooking wine." It is inferior. My Ah Paw's cooks always cooked with good wine, as did my father, Lo Pak Wen, who would say repeatedly, "If you cannot drink it, don't cook with it."

Another discovery that you will make relates to the chemistry of the Chinese kitchen. From recipe to recipe, often you will find that ingredients for a sauce, marinade, or even for cooking processes seem repetitious. But what makes Chinese cooking unique is how differently these ingredients react in combination when added and cooked in a precise order. Sameness results in variety.

As you go through the recipes you will find the chicken to be most accommodating, so long as you treat her with care and respect her taste. *"Ho ho sik,"* the Chinese say. Eat well.

Kitchen Tools, Techniques, and Processes

*T*he equipment necessary for the Chinese kitchen is minimal, simple to use, and inexpensive. Once mastered, these tools and the methods in which they are used will be a delight. Let me give you an example. Here is what you need to cook authentically in the Chinese manner.

TOOLS

 WOK This all-purpose cook pot is as much a part of Chinese culture as the Great Wall, and has remained unchanged for thousands of years. First made of iron, later of carbon steel, still later of stainless steel and aluminum, its concave shape places its round bottom right into the flame or heat source of a stove and makes it the ideal cooker.

A carbon steel wok is as perfect a cooking utensil as can be. It conducts heat virtually instantaneously. Though it is neither a pot nor a pan in the usual sense, it functions as such. The shape of a wok permits food to be stir-fried, tossed quickly through small amounts of oil so that food cooks yet does not retain oil. The wok is ideal for blanching and braising food as well.

The most useful carbon steel wok, the one I recommend most highly, is one with a diameter of about 14 inches. It is all-purpose, used for stir-frying, deep-frying, dry-roasting, and sauce making. With the addition of bamboo steamers it is also perfect for all manner of steaming. A carbon steel wok costs little and will be perfect when properly seasoned. A well-seasoned wok behaves very much like a nonstick pan. The more you use it, and the older and the more seasoned it becomes, the less oil is needed to cook.

Many other kinds of woks are available, made of stainless steel, aluminum, and various thicknesses of iron. None of these will perform as well as a seasoned carbon steel wok and all are far more expensive. (A stainless steel wok does work well in steaming.) Nor do I favor nonstick coated woks, the direct, intense heat can harm the finish and their heat cannot be controlled. No wok is as versatile as one of carbon steel. A flat-bottomed wok, of whatever material, is not recommended either, for foods cannot be whisked through it as smoothly as through one that is concave.

A carbon steel wok, when new, is coated with a sticky oil used as protection and a preservative. Once cleansed of this coating and seasoned, it is the ideal cooking pot and will last many years. A new wok should be immersed in extremely hot water with a small amount of liquid detergent, the inside cleaned with a sponge and the outside scrubbed with steel wool and cleanser. Then, after rinsing but still wet, it should be placed over a flame and dried with a paper towel to prevent rust. Discard the paper towel and, with the wok still over the burner, tip a teaspoon of oil into its bowl and rub it around with another paper towel. Repeat this oiling process until the paper towel is free of any traces of black residue. The wok is then ready for use. A new wok absorbs oil until it is properly seasoned. Once seasoned, very little oil is necessary to cook in it. After the first washing, detergents should never be used in the bowl of the wok. It should be scrubbed only in extremely hot water with a stiff-bristled wok brush. After rinsing, it should be dried with a paper towel, then placed over a flame for thorough drying. When you have finished cooking with it, re-season it with a very small amount of peanut oil rubbed around inside of the bowl with a paper towel. Repeat this for the first fifteen to twenty uses, until the wok bowl becomes shiny and dark-colored, which will indicate that it is well seasoned.

 WOK COVER This cover, 12 to 13 inches in diameter, with a top handle, is usually made of aluminum. It nestles firmly into the wok, enabling the wok to be used for stews, for steaming, and for boiling. Stainless steel covers are adequate as well.

 WOK BRUSH This wooden brush is oar-shaped, slightly oversized, with long stiff bristles. It is used with extremely hot water to remove all cooking residue from the seasoned wok.

 WOK RING This is a hollow steel base that fits over a single stove burner. The round base of the wok settles into it, keeping the wok stable and ensuring that flames from the burner will surround the wok evenly.

CHINESE SPATULA Available either in hammered carbon steel or stainless steel and in different sizes, with a flat, shovel-shaped scoop at the end of a long handle. A carbon steel spatula is of one molded piece, the scoop is about 4 inches across. A steel spatula is about the same size, with the scoop and handle of a single piece of steel. The carbon steel spatula will become seasoned with use, and I prefer it, but it has become somewhat hard to find. A stainless steel spatula is an acceptable substitute.

 CHINESE LADLE Made of stainless steel, bowl-shaped, with the bowl and its long handle fashioned from a single piece of steel, and a wood inset at its end. These ladles come in various sizes, but one about 15 inches long with a bowl from 4 to 4½ inches in diameter is perfect for all uses.

 CHINESE STRAINERS One kind of strainer is circular, made of woven steel mesh and attached to a long handle of split bamboo. It comes in many sizes, from as small as a person's palm to as large as 14 inches in diameter. For all-purpose use I prefer one 10 inches in diameter. The second kind of strainer is a rather large and shallow stainless steel bowl at the end of a hollow handle, and is made by punching round holes in the bowl. This, too, comes in a 10-inch size, which I recommend.

 BAMBOO STEAMERS These circular frames of bamboo with woven bamboo mesh bases and covers come in various sizes, but those from 12 to 13 inches in diameter are preferred because they sit perfectly in the well of the wok. Foods rest on the woven bamboo, and steam passes upward through the spaces and into the food. These steamers can be stacked two to three high so that different foods may be steamed simultaneously. Steamers are also made of aluminum, stainless steel, and wood, with bamboo mesh bases. All of these steamers are often used to serve steamed foods. Bamboo steamer sets consist of two steamers, which can be stacked, as well as a cover.

In Chinese or Asian cooking supply markets, you can find steaming sets of stainless steel. These consist of a base pot, with a cover, into which two steamers are set, one of them with a base of crosshatched steel strips, the other of bamboo interwoven strips. This set is valuable for those with limited storage space, because the set's base is an 8-quart pot, useful on its own. The same set comes in aluminum with components that are slightly larger. I prefer the steel.

Also useful for steaming are the steel insets that fit into pots and are usually used for steaming such foods as asparagus, corn, and pasta. Clam steamers substitute well, too, and many 8-quart pots come with strainer insets that can be used to steam food.

Alternatively, the wok itself can be a steamer. Simply set a cake rack firmly into the wok bowl, place the food in a steamproof dish, and set the dish on the rack. Cover with a wok cover and steam.

菜
刀

CHINESE CLEAVER Like the wok, an all-purpose tool for the Chinese kitchen is the cleaver. It cuts, dices, slices, and minces. Its flat blade and its handle can mash. Usually made of carbon steel with a wood handle, it is also available in stainless steel, either with a wood handle or with a blade and handle of one continuous piece of steel. The blades of cleavers are rounded at their ends. They come in different sizes and weights, from 12 ounces to 2 pounds. I prefer a 12-ounce stainless steel cleaver with a wood handle, the blade about 8 inches long and 3½ inches wide, a professional cleaver made by Dexter in the United States. I think it is superior for slicing, cutting, dicing, or mincing and it should be used only for those purposes.

A heavier cleaver made of carbon steel with a wood handle and weighing one pound with a 8¼ by 4-inch blade is ideal for cutting up a whole chicken and chopping its meat and bones. Often those using a cleaver for the first time are fearful that they might cut off a finger (or two). That should be of no concern. When held correctly so that its weight and balance are properly distributed, the cleaver can do virtually anything a handful of lesser knives can. It slices, shreds, dices, and hacks, all with ease. It also scoops and functions quite well as a dough scraper. When the cleaver is held properly, the weight will do the work.

Two grips are helpful: to chop and mince, in particular for the minced chicken recipes in this book, grasp the handle in a fistlike grip and swing it straight down. The strokes should be long and forceful if cutting something thick such as a chicken cutlet. When mincing, the strokes are short, rapid, and controlled. The wrist dictates the force.

To slice, dice, and shred, grip the handle as you would to chop, but permit your index finger to stretch out alongside of the blade. This provides guidance. The wrist, which barely moves with this grip, is virtually rigid and becomes almost an extension of the cleaver as the blade is drawn across the food being cut. Your other hand should anchor the food being cut, with the knuckles guiding the blade. (The blade will brush your knuckles slightly as it moves across the food.)

To flatten, hold the handle of the cleaver tightly in the same grip as for chopping. With the flat of the blade, come down hard on food that you want flattened, such as garlic, ginger, scallions, and leeks. To mash, use the cleaver handle. Hold it firmly with the index finger and thumb where it meets the blade, and clench the other fingers. The handle thus becomes a hammer that can be used, like a mortar and pestle, to make a paste such as a fermented black bean and garlic paste.

These days electric food processors and mixers are common. Slicing and chopping can be done in a processor if you wish, but I find that using a food processor removes moisture from foods and they dry out and lose their taste. I prefer the control I can exert with my hand on the cleaver and the uniformity of size that I can maintain, a characteristic important in preparing Chinese food. Once you have practiced and become adept at using the cleaver, you will prefer it as well.

CUTTING BOARDS The best for Chinese cooking are those of a rubberized composition sold in Chinese and Asian cooking supply stores. These beige to yellow boards are round, square, or rectangular, of various sizes, and are quite heavy. Their advantage is that they will never warp and are used in all professional Chinese kitchens because they are dense and their surface is easy to scour clean and will not dull the blades of cleavers. If you cannot obtain one of these, I suggest a cutting board of wood. Wood does not dull blade edges.

I do not recommend cutting boards made of opaque white plastic, since they tend to dull blades quite easily. Whichever cutting board you choose, however, clean it thoroughly after use with hot water and detergent. I stress this particularly when it comes to working with chicken.

CHOPSTICKS Bamboo chopsticks, in addition to being the basic eating utensil of the Chinese, are excellent cooking tools. With them you may mix, stir, and serve. They come usually in packages of ten. Avoid plastic chopsticks, which should never be used for cooking and are more difficult to manipulate than bamboo when eating. Chopsticks, are you might expect, are decorative as well and come in a variety of materials—ivory, jade, teak, ebony and palisander woods, gold and silver. In one imperial court, according to a bit of folklore, ivory chopsticks were used exclusively to test foods for poison, for ivory tended to blacken if touched by poison.

To complete your Chinese kitchen you will also need:

Frying pan, cast iron, 10 inches in diameter
Nonstick skillet, 10 inches in diameter
Round cake pan, 9 inches in diameter
Selection of tempered dishes for steaming

Selection of stainless steel dishes for steaming
Mesh strainer (all-purpose)
Small single panel hand grater
Garlic press
Kitchen shears
Cooking thermometer (for deep-frying)

Once you have added these Chinese cooking tools to your kitchen, you should use them to your advantage. The techniques for using these tools are as simple as the tools themselves. So much of the success in Chinese cooking depends upon proper use of equipment and adding the proper ingredients in their proper order.

TECHNIQUES

 STIR-FRYING The aim of stir-frying is to cook foods to the point at which they retain their flavors, colors, textures, and nutritive values. All these elements are essential to any good cooking. All foods to be stir-fried should be cut to sizes indicated and placed in a spot convenient to the wok. Sauces should be mixed and ready as well. This is simply organization, so that as you cook, everything will be within reach and the rhythm of the stir-fry will not be interrupted. The best stir-fried foods are those that retain their essence while at the same time absorbing and retaining the heat of the wok.

The stir-fry is surely the most dramatic of all Chinese cooking techniques. Hands and arms move in rhythm as foods are whisked through oil. When I am ready to stir-fry, I heat the wok for a specific time, usually 30 seconds or more. Temperature is most important when stir-frying. I pour oil into the wok and coat its insides by spreading the oil with my spatula. The wok is ready to use when a wisp of white smoke can be seen rising from the oil. Another test is to drop a slice of ginger into the oil; when it turns light brown the oil is ready.

When I want to stir-fry chicken, I first cut it into uniform pieces, usually bite-size, before cooking. As you will see with the individual recipes, chicken morsels should generally be placed in the oiled wok in a thin single layer, cooked for a specified time, then turned over and stirred briefly. At this point the chicken will be cooked to about 70 percent of doneness. When the accompanying ingredients, usually vegetables, are added and stir-fried, the chicken is cooked through.

When cooking vegetables, I usually add a bit of salt to the oil to bring out their flavors. I occasionally blanch vegetables if they tend to be very firm. Place what is to be cooked in the wok and begin tossing them through the oil with the spatula, 1 to 2 minutes for soft vegetables such as bok choy and scallions, perhaps a minute longer for firmer vegetables such as cabbage, carrots, and broccoli. Scoop out the vegetables and serve.

Cooking on a gas range is best for Chinese food because of the range's greater heat and the height of its flame, particularly for stir-fries that require direct, high heat. There is a technique, however, for obtaining high heat as well as necessary variance using an electric range. It is a method I devised and one that I teach with success: I use two electric burners, side by side. I turn one burner to its highest setting and allow it to heat for 10 minutes. After 5 minutes, I turn the other burner to medium. Place the wok on the highest heat and allow it to heat for 1 to 1½ minutes, until the wok is very hot. At this point add the oil, and when a wisp of white smoke appears the wok is ready. Place the food in the wok. If it begins to cook too quickly or looks as if it is about to burn, move the wok to the burner on medium heat. Move the wok back and forth between burners as necessary. Once you have become accustomed to this technique you will cook Chinese foods perfectly without a gas range and with ease.

As a general rule, never double a recipe for stir-frying unless you have a range of restaurant quality. Otherwise, cook in two batches, or the heat will be inadequate.

DEEP-FRYING To deep-fry is not to simply plunge foods into boiling oil. Proper deep-frying should produce foods cooked thoroughly inside, yet moist, while outside they are golden, tender, or lightly crusted. Correct temperatures are important, for if the oil is not at a precise temperature the oil will permeate the food rather than cook it well. The taste of oil should never dominate.

When I want to make a wok into a deep-fryer, I heat it briefly, pour in the required amount of cooking oil (usually 4 to 6 cups), and heat it to 325° to 375° F, depending on what is being cooked. The individual recipe for chicken will determine the oil temperature. In general the oil should be heated to a few degrees higher than required because when the food is added, the oil temperature will drop before rising again. Use a frying thermometer, which is placed in the oil, to maintain proper temperature. When the proper temperature has been reached, slide the food into the oil.

The best utensil for deep-frying is the Chinese mesh strainer. Its large surface and stout bamboo handle are ideal for removing foods from oil and straining them as well. The strainer is far more useful than a slotted spoon.

 OIL-BLANCHING This simple cooking technique is basically a sealing process. The aim is to retain flavor, color, and moisture in the food. Heat the wok, add the required amount of cooking oil, and heat the oil to 300° F (the temperature will vary with individual recipes). Vegetables should usually be blanched for no longer than 30 to 45 seconds, then removed and drained with a mesh strainer. Chicken usually requires longer blanching times, depending upon the individual recipe. It is most important that after oil-blanching, the food be thoroughly drained.

 WATER-BLANCHING This process removes water from vegetables. It is an odd concept that to remove water you place vegetables in water, but it works. Pour 3 to 4 cups of water into a wok, add ¼ teaspoon of baking soda, and bring to a boil. (The baking soda is optional; it ensures a bright color for whichever vegetable is blanched.) Place the vegetables in the water. When their color becomes bright, usually no more than 30 seconds, remove them, place them in a bowl, and run cold water over them to halt the cooking process. Alternatively, the vegetables may be placed in a bowl of cold water with ice cubes. Drain well.

Occasionally foods may be blanched in stock. Simply heat stock in a wok, usually 1 to 2 cups, until boiling. Place the food in stock for 10 to 30 seconds, depending upon the recipe. Remove and drain well. I cannot stress enough that all blanched foods must be drained thoroughly.

 DRY-ROASTING With this process there is no need for oil, salt, or anything else in the wok except the food to be roasted. I dry-roast nuts and sesame seeds to enhance their flavor. To dry-roast nuts, heat the wok over high heat for 30 to 45 seconds. Add the nuts, lower the heat to very low, and spread the nuts in a single layer, moving them around with your spatula to prevent burning. The process takes 12 to 15 minutes, or until the nuts brown. When browned, remove from the wok and allow to cool. Use the same process for sesame seeds, but roast for only 2 minutes.

 STEAMING Steaming foods in the Chinese manner gives them life and preserves their natural flavor. Dry foods become moist, breads become softened, and foods that have shrunk, expand. Steaming bestows a glistening coating of moisture. It is artful as well, because foods can be arranged attractively within a bamboo steamer, and once steamed can be served directly from the steamer. Steaming requires no oil, except the small amount that is brushed on the woven bamboo base of the steamer to prevent sticking.

To steam, pour 2 quarts of water into a wok and bring to a boil. Place the steamer in the wok so that it will sit evenly above, but not touching, the water. (You will be able to stack two steamers, or more, should you wish.) Cover the top steamer. Boiling water should be on hand at all times during the steaming process to replenish any that evaporates from the wok. Steaming times vary with the foods in individual recipes. As mentioned earlier, there are alternative steamers available. In general, if your foods are in metal dishes in the steamer, they will cook more quickly than if they were in tempered porcelain or Pyrex dishes. And though there are metal steamers, pots, and steaming insets, I recommend the traditional bamboo steamer for best results.

TEMPERING DISHES FOR STEAMING Porcelain or Pyrex dishes may be used inside steamers, but first they should be tempered and seasoned. Some think that it is unnecessary to temper Pyrex because it is tempered glass. This is only true for Pyrex that is used in the oven. It has been my experience, and that of my students, that Pyrex may indeed crack during steaming. So it is best to temper Pyrex along with porcelain. The process is quick, simple, and much safer.

Here is how to temper: fill a wok with 5 to 6 cups of cold water. Place a cake rack in the wok and stack the dishes to be tempered on the rack, making certain they are completely covered with the cold water. Cover with the wok cover and bring the water to a boil. Allow the water to boil for 10 minutes, turn off the heat and allow the wok to cool to room temperature. The dishes are now seasoned and can be placed in steamers without fear that they will crack. The dishes may also be used in place of steamers. Foods are placed in the seasoned, tempered, steamproof dishes, which are in turn placed on racks within the wok. Once tempered, these dishes will remain so for their lifetime.

SELECTING AND PREPARING THE CHICKEN

The terms "free-range chickens" and "organic chickens" were foreign to me when I came to the United States. Chickens in the small village of Siu Lo Chen were always free running and living off the land. Even in Hong Kong, live chickens were brought in fresh daily from poultry raisers in the New Territories and in

China. I learned, when I came to America, that most of the poultry sold was not freshly killed, a practice unknown to me. Nor were so-called chicken "parts" ever offered in China. One bought a chicken, a whole chicken, killed it or had it killed, and prepared it.

Today it is possible to find markets that deal in live poultry, though they are rare. Let me say that there is truly no substitute for the taste of a chicken freshly killed and cooked. To seek out live chicken markets—usually to be found in ethnically defined areas where immigrants and their descendants cling to traditional shopping and eating habits—is worth the effort. If possible find birds that have been hand plucked. Otherwise they probably have been plunged into boiling water to make their feathers easier to remove by machine. This diminishes their taste.

However, because fresh-killed chickens are not common and most people buy their chickens already processed, let me make some suggestions. I strongly recommend chickens that have been raised in a free-range way, and those that have been organically fed. Though such claims abound these days, it is worth the effort to check on the pedigrees of your chickens and to shop in the markets that you trust.

Always seek out fresh birds and avoid those that have been processed. In these times of packaged chickens and packaged chicken parts, be certain you check the dates on the packages. If the date is past, do not buy the chicken. Also check to see if the chicken has been frozen; often chickens are delivered frozen and permitted to defrost in refrigerated cases. Avoid frozen chickens if possible. To test the chicken, press the flesh of the packaged bird; if it is hard or there are traces of crystallization on or around it, do not buy it.

If a chicken has been in a display case for too long, the package is liable to contain an excess of reddish, blood-colored liquid. Do not buy that bird, either.

Some chickens are never frozen but are delivered to markets fresh daily. Seek these out. I might even urge you to become friends with your butcher and perhaps he will ensure that when these cold, fresh birds come in, he will save one or more for you.

I suggest that if you are buying whole chicken breasts, have your butcher cut them from a fresh chicken. For chicken cutlets, which are simply breasts that have been boned, have him do the same. A good market and a good butcher will be happy to oblige.

Cleaning a Chicken

Before you work with a whole chicken you must clean it thoroughly. Simply follow these steps: place the chicken in a sink and run cold water into its cavity to wash away the blood and liquid residue. Run water around the outside to clean the skin. Remove the fat and membranes, which are in the rear and neck cavities. (At the rear there will be a large piece, or pieces, of chicken fat. Remove these but do not discard them. They may be frozen for later use. In this book you will find uses for chicken fat.)

Run cold water in and out of the chicken to rid it of any residual pieces. Sprinkle the outside of the chicken with ¼ cup of salt, rubbing it well into the skin and flesh. Rinse the salt off. The skin will be clear and quite smooth to the touch. Drain the chicken by sitting it, rear down, in a mesh strainer over a bowl. Pat dry with paper towels. The chicken is now ready to be prepared.

Cutting Up a Whole Chicken

Most people buy their chickens already cut up. It is better, as I have noted, to purchase a whole chicken, clean it, and cut it up yourself. Cutting up a chicken is simple. Here is the procedure: sit the bird up on its neck, its back to you, its tail and legs up. Using the cleaver, cut downward from the spinal joint. As you cut through, use your hands to pull the chicken apart. With the cleaver, cut the center joint of the breast bone. The chicken is now cut into halves. Cut off the thighs and wings at their joints. Cut each half of the body into halves lengthwise, then cut these lengths into bite-size pieces. This procedure is identical for both uncooked and cooked chickens.

The chicken is now ready to be prepared or, if already cooked, to be eaten.

In these days of chicken in parts, breasts, thighs, legs, and wings are sold separately. Once, your butcher would cut up a chicken for you and present the parts ready to cook, even the necks and innards for soups and stocks. He would cut breasts from a whole chicken and bone them for you, creating chicken cutlets, which are simply breasts with bones and cartilage removed. Unfortunately in these times such service seems to be, if not a lost art, surely a lost service. To be sure, some butchers will cut up a chicken for you, but not too many. Therefore, it would be wise for you to know how to bone a breast to create chicken cutlets without waste.

In the recipes in this book I refer to chicken breasts and to chicken cutlets.

Chicken breasts are always whole breasts, by weight, with skin and bones intact. Chicken cutlets are the breast meat, by weight, without skin and bones.

Boning a Chicken Breast

As with a whole chicken, a breast—or any other chicken part that comes with skin and some membrane—should be washed thoroughly, sprinkled with 1 to 2 tablespoons of salt, rubbed, and rinsed again. As you would with a whole chicken drain the part and dry with paper towels.

To bone a chicken breast and make it a cutlet, do the following: lay the breast, bone side up, on a work surface. Use a cleaver to make a cut in the top of the breastbone adjacent to the wishbone. With your hands, bend the halves, which will break easily, exposing the cartilage. Then, with a boning knife or small sharp knife, separate the meat from the cartilage by cutting the meat and pulling it away from the cartilage. With your knife, gently separate the breast from the rib bones. The meat will come away from the bones very easily. Work until the breast meat is free of bone. Repeat with the other half of the breast. The chicken breast, now boned and in two pieces, is ready for use.

When working with uncooked chicken, it is wise to be especially clean. Wash any work surface with soap and hot water, and do the same with any equipment you have used to process your chicken. Finally, wash your hands with soap and hot water.

Chinese Ingredients
and Essentials

*T*here was a time when most of the foods, surely most of the ingredients, of Chinese cooking were considered exotic and mysterious. People liked to eat Chinese food, but they were essentially ignorant of what they ate. This was equally true of professionals who would often attempt to explain Chinese food, then would give up in frustration. Times have changed. Through exposure and travel, and because of the work of myself and others, people have become more knowledgeable about most of the foods of the Chinese table. It is not at all unusual these days to find an assortment of soy sauces, rice wine vinegars, sesame seed oils, and hoisins on supermarket shelves, along with all manner of Chinese noodles and packages, bottles, and cans of Chinese vegetables and condiments. Even though there is a variety of Chinese foods, their tastes have become more widely known and accepted by the Western palate.

With this familiarity and recognition has come more extensive use, with more and more people, including professional cooks, shopping for foods in Chinese and other Asian markets. Virtually every market, whether it is large or small, has shelves stocked with Chinese ingredients. This, too, is a happy circumstance.

Very few of the foods in this book are not available widely. Most can be found in your local market or in Chinese or Asian markets. Most of the spices, oils, condiments, soy sauces, and wines are of Chinese origin and are imported from the People's Republic of China, Hong Kong, Taiwan, and the countries of Southeast Asia, and Japan. A great many of these foods are available by mail order, and through the Internet, particularly those dried, preserved, pickled, bottled, and canned.

For this book, I have made a point of using traditional spices, sauces, and foods that enhance the taste of chicken. I am confident you will enjoy working with them and perhaps discovering them. I caution you to refrain from using such

prepared ingredients as those in bottles labeled "stir-fry sauces," and "wok oils," as well as so-called "sweet and sour" or "Sichuan," "sparerib" sauces. In no way do they approximate the true tastes of Chinese preparations.

In this book, in addition to ingredients that are authentic and available, you will find a small collection of recipes for foods and ingredients that are used over and over in my recipes. These are my own, which I think are essentials. In addition, I offer substitutes, where possible, for ingredients that might be difficult to obtain.

Brands of Asian products have also proliferated. I refrain from recommending brands except when I believe one in particular is far superior to others and thus, in my view, essential to the taste of the recipe. A note of caution: there is quite a bit of fanciful and imprecise labeling on Chinese ingredients, with one often being labeled differently by different processors. It can be bewildering. I have taken pains to list these variations. Read them with care. A suggestion I make always is to take photocopies of the ingredients you need, along with their Chinese calligraphy, and present them to your shopkeeper. It helps immeasurably. I cannot urge you more strongly to do this, for in the end it will add to your enjoyment.

 BAMBOO SHOOTS The pale yellow, pear-shaped young beginnings of bamboo. Once, fresh bamboo shoots were unavailable outside Asia, and those that did reach markets were usually dried and discolored. This is no longer the case. Fresh bamboo shoots are sometimes available in Chinese groceries but are tough and must be boiled before use. Winter bamboo shoots are generally deemed most desirable because they are more tender and less fibrous. More widely available are canned shoots, and they are labeled "winter bamboo shoots" or "bamboo shoots, tips." They are canned as large chunks or as smaller pieces, sliced or julienned. I prefer the large chunks so they can be cut as desired. Once a can is opened, the shoots must be transferred to another container. They will keep, refrigerated and in a closed container, for 2 to 3 weeks if the water is changed daily.

 BEAN CURD This fresh, versatile foodstuff, called *daufu* by the Chinese and tofu by the Japanese, comes in cakes 2½ to 3 inches square. They are occasionally sold in bulk in water in some Asian markets but are usually packaged. These custard-like cakes, made from a soybean liquid product called "milk," are preferable to packages or to the large blocks that are often sold. Bean curd has little taste of its own. Its versatility lies in its ability to absorb the tastes of the foods with which it is combined. It will keep for up to 2 weeks refrigerated in water in a closed container, with the water changed daily. Fresh bean curd is usually sold in three distinct textures—soft, firm, and extra firm.

 BEAN SPROUTS When bean sprouts are mentioned in this book, the reference is to mung bean sprouts, which are plump with a distinctive crunch. They are sold by weight in markets. Stored in the refrigerator in water in a closed container, they will keep for up to 4 days, after which they soften and become colorless. Another variety of bean sprout is the soybean sprout, also white, but longer than mung bean sprouts with yellow baby soybeans at their tips. They are stronger in taste and should not be substituted for mung bean sprouts.

 BEAN THREAD NOODLES Often labeled "bean threads," "vermicelli bean threads," or "cellophane noodles," they are made with mung beans that are moistened, mashed, strained, and formed into very thin white noodles. They come dried, in 1/2-pound packages, divided into eight 2-ounce bundles. Avoid other large packages of regularly shaped, carelessly formed sheets and long, thick, rough sticks, which are made with soybeans and should not be confused with bean thread noodles. Both are usually labeled "dried bean thread" and are sandy brown in color.

 BLACK BEANS, FERMENTED These fragrant black beans preserved in salt come either in plastic sacks or wrapped cardboard packages. The beans are cooked and lightly flavored with ginger and orange peel. Before use the salt must be rinsed off. They will keep for up to a year without refrigeration, in a tightly sealed container.

 BOK CHOY Surely China's most popular and most widely recognized vegetable. It's name translates as "white vegetable" because of its white bulbous stalk, which contrasts with its deep green leaves. It is crisp and sweet, and though often referred to as "Chinese cabbage," it bears no resemblance to cabbage. Bok choy will keep for about a week in the vegetable drawer of a refrigerator, but because it tends to lose its sweetness quickly I recommend using it within two to three days.

 BOK CHOY, SHANGHAI These are smaller than bok choy, with pronounced bulbous stalks. They are often called *ching bok choy,* which means literally "greenish

white vegetable," an apt name because its stalks are less white than bok choy and its leaves less green. If you ask for Shanghai bok choy you may be looked at strangely. Ask for *tong choy* and there will be no problem. Like bok choy, it should be stored in a refrigerated vegetable drawer and used at its freshest because it softens as it ages.

CHILIES, THAI These are my chilies of choice. Small and thin, colored deep red to deep green, about 1½ inches long, they are quite hot. They impart a heat that tends to linger in the mouth yet are quite pleasant. I find them dependable in terms of the numbers needed to achieve desired hotness. They will keep, refrigerated, for about 4 weeks in an open container, covered lightly with plastic wrap. Do not seal the container or the chilies will deteriorate. Dried Thai chilies can be used as well, but their heat will be less intense.

CHINESE BLACK MUSHROOMS These dried mushrooms, black, dark gray, or speckled in color, comes in boxes or cellophane packs. Their caps range in size from about the width of a nickel to 3 inches in diameter. Those in boxes are the choicest in size and color, and are priced accordingly. They are the same mushrooms known as shiitake outside of China. These mushrooms must always be soaked in hot water for at least a half hour before use, their stems removed and discarded, and thoroughly cleaned on the undersides of the caps and squeezed dry. In their dried form they will keep indefinitely at room temperature in a tightly closed container. If you live in an especially damp or humid climate, they should be stored in the freezer. I prefer the dried mushrooms over the fresh because of the concentrated intensity of their flavor.

CHINESE CHIVES These are also known as garlic chives. More pungent than the chives known in the West, and wider and flatter, they are the same deep green color. Yellow chives are the same vegetable, but as they grow they are deprived of the sun and thus become a lighter color. Green chives taste like garlic, yellow chives like onion. If you cannot find Chinese chives you may substitute customary chives but the taste of the dish will be different.

CLOUD EARS These brown or brown-black dried fungi look a bit like round chips. When soaked in water, as they must be for use, they soften and glisten and resemble flower petals. Dry, they keep indefinitely in a closed jar kept in a cool, dry place. Cloud ears used to be interchangeable with "tree ears," also known as wood ears, a brownish fungus that also grows on wood. Cloud ears, however, are smaller and more tender and I greatly prefer them.

CORIANDER This aromatic leaf is also called fresh coriander, to distinguish it from coriander seed. It is also called Chinese parsley and in the southwestern United States is known as cilantro. It is similar to parsley only in appearance. Coriander has an intense fragrance and imparts a distinctive taste when used either as a flavoring or a garnish. Although some suggest that Italian parsley may be used as a substitute, it may not. The flavors and aromas are completely different. There is no substitute for coriander. It should be used fresh but can be kept in the refrigerator for a week.

CURRY POWDER A blend of spices that can include turmeric, cumin, fennel, and coriander seeds. There are many brands of curry powder on the market but I prefer the stronger, more pungent brands from India and Malaysia.

EGGPLANT, CHINESE This bright lavender to purple eggplant, often tinged with white, is narrower than its Western counterpart, usually no wider than 2 inches in diameter at its thickest. Its taste is that of usual eggplant, but its skin is quite tender and need not be removed before cooking.

EIGHT-STAR ANISE This is also called star anise. It is a tiny, hard, eight-pointed star fruit of the Chinese anise tree. It is a most intense spice, with a flavor more pronounced than that of anise seed. It should be used sparingly. Stored in a tightly sealed jar kept in a cool, dry place, it will keep for a year, though it may gradually lose its intensity.

FIVE-SPICE SEASONING The five spices in this mix can be any combination of five of the following: star anise, fennel seeds, cinnamon, cloves, ginger, licorice, nutmeg, and Sichuan peppercorns. Different brands use different mixtures, though anise and cinnamon usually dominate. You may devise your own five-spice seasoning by asking for a mix at a Chinese herbal shop. The herbalist will be only too happy to oblige. Often the spices are ground into a powder that is quite pungent and should be used sparingly.

FLOURS There are many brands of flour available, and it is common knowledge that flours react to climate and temperature. After meticulous trial and error, I have chosen three as ideal for the doughs of the breads and buns in this book. Individual recipes call for specific flours:

Pillsbury Best Bread Flour, enriched bromide, naturally white, high protein, high gluten

Pillsbury Best All-Purpose Flour, enriched, bleached

Gold Medal All-Purpose Flour, enriched, bleached

 GINGER These often gnarled, irregular roots are also referred to as ginger root. When selecting them, look for those with smooth outer skins, because ginger begins to wrinkle and roughen with age. It flavors extremely well. It should be used sparingly and should be sliced, and often peeled, before use. Its strength is indicated by its preparation, which I specify in each recipe: sliced, peeled or unpeeled, smashed lightly, julienned, minced, shredded. Placed in a heavy brown paper bag and refrigerated it will keep for 4 to 5 weeks.

 GINGER JUICE This is an ingredient that is best made fresh. Peel a 2-inch piece of ginger and using a small single panel grater, grate into a small bowl. Place the grated ginger in a garlic press and squeeze into a small bowl. This will yield about a tablespoon. Ginger juice once was available in jars, but it is hard to find.

 HOISIN SAUCE A thick, chocolate-brown, sweetened sauce made from soybeans, garlic, sugar, and chilies. Some brands add a little vinegar to the mix; others thicken the sauce with flour. Often it is mistakenly called "plum sauce." Hoisin comes in jars. Once opened, it must be refrigerated. It will keep for at least 6 months.

 HOT PEPPER OIL There are many brands of hot pepper oil on market shelves. Unfortunately, either their strengths differ or they are made from inferior oils, so it is preferable to make your own (see page 40). I use a peanut oil base. You will have, as a by-product of the oil, hot pepper flakes at the bottom of the oil, which you can use repeatedly.

JICAMA More familiar to the Chinese as *sah gut,* this bulbous root is sweet and crisp, with a sand-colored exterior and white interior. It can be eaten raw or cooked. Its name reflects its Western origin, but it has become widely cultivated in China and the rest of Asia. It is fine on its own, but is an admirable substitute for water chestnuts. Stored in a brown paper bag and refrigerated, jicama will keep for 3 to 4 days.

KETCHUP Like its Western counterpart, ketchup from China comes in bottles. The best brand, Koon Yick Wan Kee, comes from Hong Kong and is made from tomatoes, vinegar, and spices. In Chinese cooking, ketchup is used as a coloring agent rather than a flavor. It is believed by some that ketchup originated in China. In southern China, on the island of Amoy, a mix of fish essence and soy sauce called *keh chap* has been suggested as the original ketchup. Chinese ketchup is not widely available, and if you cannot find it Western ketchup can be substituted.

 LOTUS LEAVES (OR BAMBOO LEAVES) The large, dried leaves are used as wrappers and flavor enhancers, usually in various steamed preparations. Lotus leaves impart a distinctive, somewhat sweet taste to the foods they are wrapped around and are preferable to bamboo leaves. Both are sold in plastic-wrapped packages by weight. Bamboo leaves are adequate substitutes but their smell and taste is less defined. These leaves, kept in plastic in a dry place, will keep from 6 months to a year.

 MALTOSE Also called malt sugar, this thick syrup is made by the reaction of enzymes with starches such as wheat flour. It is pleasantly sweet, and when mixed with vinegar and boiling water it is used to coat chicken skin before roasting. It is packaged in small plastic containers and may be stored in these containers, in a cool, dark place. The longer it is kept, the harder it becomes, though it will not spoil, so it should not be kept for an extended period.

 MUSTARD, HOT This is made by mixing equal amounts of dry mustard powder and cold tap water. There are many mustard powders on the market, but I prefer the English-made Coleman's Mustard, Double Superfine Compound. Look for the dried mustard powder, not the Coleman's prepared mustard that comes in jars.

 NOODLES There are many variations on the noodle in China, all of them known collectively as *mein* or *min*. Because of their flour base, other foods made from doughs are often called "noodle fruit." There are wheat flour noodles, fresh and dried, of various widths, made either with just water, or with eggs added. There are rice noodles, also fresh and dried, of various widths. Very fine rice noodles are called rice sticks. (There is even a rice noodle that is not a noodle, though it is called rice noodle [see page 29.]) There are mung bean noodles, bean thread noodles (see page 23) and a type that is shaped like linguine and needs only to be soaked in hot water to use.

I list the preferred type of noodle in each recipe. For most recipes fine vermicelli or capellini pasta, fresh or dried, will substitute quite well, though it is preferable to use the traditional Chinese noodle.

OILS Peanut oil is the preferred oil of the Chinese kitchen, not only for its healthy attributes but for the distinctive nutty flavor it imparts. I have also used peanut oil to create a group of flavored infused oils for specific recipes. These are detailed in each recipe. For all of the recipes in this book, however, soybean, corn, or canola oil may be substituted.

OYSTER SAUCE The base of this rich condiment is ground oysters that have been boiled and dried and then cooked with water, salt, and starch into a molasses-like thickness. It is a highly prized seasoning in China, not only for its distinctive taste but also for its color. It is well regarded by Buddhists because the oyster is a permitted seafood in their vegetarian diets, along with clams and mussels. Once opened, a bottle of oyster sauce should be refrigerated and will keep indefinitely. The preferred brand, widely available, is Hop Sing Lung, made in Hong Kong. If unavailable, another brand, Lee Kum Kee, may be used.

PRESERVED VEGETABLE These are preserved mustard plants that have been cooked, preserved in salt and sugar, and dried. It is the necessary ingredient for beggar's chicken. The Chinese call this *mui choi*. Brown in color when dried, it is soft and pliable with a texture quite like that of prunes. It is used in steaming, stir-frying, braising, and in soups. It comes in packages labeled "preserved vegetable," but also, on occasion, "preserved mustard" or "salted mustard." If there is a question, simply ask the grocer for *mui choi*. Often tiny salt crystals will be seen on it, but they do not affect the food. It should be stored in a sealed jar kept at room temperature and will keep for up to 6 months. The longer it is kept, the darker it gets. Before use the leaves must be opened and the salt and grit thoroughly removed by washing.

RED IN SNOW This is a green leafy vegetable, similar to collard greens, that is a Shanghai favorite, but eaten all over China. Its more mundane name is snow cabbage, but in China it is known as *hseut loi hung*, or "red in snow." It is rarely eaten fresh. Usually it is water-blanched and preserved in salt. It is frequently cut up for use in soups, with noodles, or in stir-fries. It comes in small cans often labeled "snow cabbage," "Shanghai cabbage," or "pickled cabbage," but it is the same vegetable. It also comes in plastic packages labeled "red in snow."

RICE In its many forms and varieties, rice is the universal food staple of China, called *mai* when raw, *fan* when cooked. Rice is grown as short, medium, and long grain, with extra long grain the most widely used. There is a distinction in China between long-grain and extra long-grain rices, with the length of the latter being more than 4 times its width. The Chinese favor it for its elegance. Extra long-grain rice grown in Texas is very good indeed. In addition, a fragrant, extra long-grain rice from Thailand called jasmine rice is excellent. There are medium- and short-grain rices and glutinous rices that adhere when cooked. Each grain is separate when extra long-grain rice is cooked perfectly (page 37).

Black and red rices are available as well, with red rice used mainly as a coloring agent by the Fujian, Chiu Chow, and Hakka people of southern China. Brown rice is simply rice that has been only partially milled to permit its brown chaff to remain.

Rice is boiled, steamed, fried, nestled into pastries and dumplings, and wrapped in leaves. Its powder is made into flour for other uses or is cooked with sugar to create a substitute for mother's milk. In this book rice is cooked on its own, as an accompaniment, or as an ingredient. For many dishes in this book, including virtually every stir-fry, I recommend cooked rice as an accompaniment. You will find glutinous rices used in congees and in other recipes.

RICE NOODLE Though this ingredient is known as *sah hor fun,* or "sand river noodle," it is not a noodle. It is made with rice flour and water and comes not in strands but rather in pliable sheets, usually square but occasionally round. Sold only in noodle factories in Chinese neighborhoods, it is snowy white with a shiny, glistening surface when fresh, and the sheets are usually oiled and folded before packaging. The sheets are cut to any size desired for use. It must be used only when fresh. It will keep only for about 3 days refrigerated, and for up to 1 to 2 months frozen. After refrigerating or freezing, it must be allowed to return to room temperature before use.

ROCK SUGAR A compound of white sugar, raw brown sugar, and honey that the Chinese call *bing tong,* or "ice sugar," it is also known as rock candy. Its taste is more elegant than that of plain white sugar, and among the older master chefs of China, rock sugar is the sweetener of choice. I recommend it as well. Available in Chinese and Asian markets, it comes in plastic packs of about a pound, and resembles a collection of small rocks and pebbles (thus its name), ranging in color from white to pale amber. If unavailable use plain white sugar.

SESAME SEEDS, BLACK AND WHITE These seeds, of either color, are customarily used as garnishes or decorations, in addition to being an ingredient. Dry-roasting them (see page 16) releases their fine aroma, which adds greatly to any dish.

SESAME OIL This aromatic oil is made from pressed, often toasted, sesame seeds. It has a defined nutlike aroma. I prefer it as an addition to sauces and marinades, as a dressing, or to finish a dish before serving. It is not recommended as a cooking oil, despite what you may have heard, for it tends to burn quickly. Adding a bit of sesame oil as a finish adds elegance to soups, for example. It is thick and brown in versions from China and Japan, thinner and lighter in versions from the Middle East. I recommend sesame oil from China. Stored in a tightly closed bottle at room temperature, it will keep for at least 4 months.

SESAME PASTE This paste is made by mixing ground white sesame seeds with soybean oil. It is known in the Middle East as tahini. It comes in jars and is smooth, with the consistency of peanut butter. The Chinese paste is thicker and richer, its sesame taste more pronounced than that of tahini. After opening, the jar should be refrigerated. It will keep for 6 months.

SHAO-HSING WINE This sherry-like wine is made and bottled in China and in Taiwan. There are several grades of differing degrees of alcohol. I use not only the basic wine but also the best refined grade of Shao-Hsing, which is labeled "Hua Tiao Chiew." You may simply ask for far jiu, a generic term, like Burgundy. Take care not to buy bottles labeled "Shao-Hsing wine for cooking," for it is inferior wine with an inferior taste. I use Shao-Hsing in marinades, sauces, or as a cooking ingredient. A dry sherry is an acceptable substitute, but again, do not use so-called cooking wine.

SICHUAN PEPPERCORNS These are neither hot nor peppery, but mild in flavor, very different from typical peppercorns. They are reddish in color and not solid, but opened, and are often called flower peppercorns. Store them in a tightly closed jar as you would ordinary peppercorns. Several recipes call for ground peppercorns. These cannot be bought; you must grind them yourself using a mortar and pestle or smash them with the broad side of a cleaver blade and then strain through a sieve. Stored in a cool place they will keep for up to 6 months.

SICHUAN PEPPERCORN PASTE This is an ingredient that you cannot buy; you must make it yourself. This fragrant paste was once a "secret" ingredient among the chefs of Sichuan, but that is no longer the case. I use it several times in this book. Here is the recipe: In a small bowl, combine 1½ teaspoons sichuan peppercorns, 1 tablespoon minced ginger, and ½ cup scallions, finely sliced. Mash them into a paste with a mortar and pestle or the handle of a cleaver. This will yield ¼ cup of paste. It should be used immediately to maximize the fragrance and will keep only for about 3 days, refrigerated.

 SILK SQUASH An odd, thin, cucumber-shaped gourd, with pronounced ridges running along its length. Its outside is deep green, but its flesh is white, faintly sweet, with a soft texture. It is excellent in soups.

 SOY SAUCE A staple of the Chinese kitchen for three thousand years, soy sauce is the product of fermented soybeans mixed with wheat flour, water, and salt. The soybean is one of the most nutritious foods in the world. A pound of soybeans contains twice the protein of the same weight of beef, more iron than a pound of beef liver, and is richer in digestible calcium than an equivalent amount of milk. In addition to being a source of other vitamins, it is extremely versatile. It is the source of soy sauce, bean curd, soybean milk, and soybean sprouts. In China, even its pods are eaten as snacks after being cooked in water and then baked over a fire.

Soy sauce comes in light and dark varieties. The light soys are usually taken from the tops of batches being fermented, generally in earthenware crocks, while the darker soys from the bottom. The best soy sauces are fermented naturally in the sun rather than in factories. Dark soys are labeled "dark" or "black," and "double dark" or "double black," the "double" soy sauce being darker and thicker. There is an even thicker and darker "pearl" sauce available. The dark soys are best for imparting a rich color to a dish. Molasses is added to some dark soys. Light soys are lighter in color and are often labeled "pure bean," "light," and "thin." The Chinese refer to light soys as *sin tin*, which translates as "fresh sweet" and means that it tends to enhance flavors of the foods in a dish. It does not mean sweet in the Western sense of the word.

I prefer the soys from Hong Kong and China to all others, including those produced in the United States and Japan, some of which lack a defined flavor, are thin in texture, and are occasionally too salty. The formula for most Chinese soys is 90 percent soybeans, and 10 percent flour for fermentation. Japanese soys are based upon a mixture of 50 percent each of soybeans and flour.

The light and dark soys I regard as superior are made in Canada as well as in Hong Kong. The best brand is Yuet Heung Yuen, originally brewed in Hong

Kong, now in British Columbia. The bottles are labeled "pure bean" for the light soy and "(C) soy" for its double dark. The second brand is made in Hong Kong's New Territories by the Koon Chun Sauce Factory. Their light soy is labeled "thin," their double dark labeled "double black." There is another soy sauce I like to use, one to which mushrooms have been added for additional sweetness. It comes from China and is labeled "Pearl River Bridge Mushroom Soy."

In the recipes in this book I specify particular soys. I stress that every effort should be made to procure the soy called for, because each affects the foods in a specific way. If I specify double dark, try to obtain it, but if you cannot, use dark. If dark is unobtainable and your market only has bottles simply labeled "soy sauce," then you may use those, but the tastes will differ.

Soys give body and richness to cooking. I often combine soys for different tastes and different colors in dishes. When used as an ingredient in recipes, soy can also be a dip. In general, the Chinese use soy more sparingly than do Westerners, many of whom I have observed pour it in large amounts over their food. Using it in that manner destroys its taste. Most soys come in bottles and sometimes in large cans. If you buy canned soy sauce, transfer it to bottles. Soy sauce can be kept in a tightly capped bottle at room temperature for up to a year.

 SUGARCANE SUGAR The other sugar of the Chinese kitchen is made from sugarcane and comes in small loaflike blocks, layered and caramel-colored. The Chinese call them *pin tong*, or "sliced sugar." They come plastic-wrapped in 1-pound packages or occasionally loose in crocks, which are sold by weight. If unavailable, use dark brown sugar as a substitute.

 TANGERINE PEEL, DRIED This dried, wrinkled brown skin of the tangerine is used for flavoring. The darker the dried peel, the older it is, and the older the better. The oldest dried tangerine peels are also the most expensive. The peels are sold in packages and can be stored indefinitely. Dry your own if you can.

 TAPIOCA STARCH Also called tapioca flour, tapioca starch is made from the starch of the cassava root. Much of it comes packaged from Thailand. It is used as a basic ingredient for doughs, for dusting or coating in many dishes, and as a thickening agent for sauces. I do not recommend that you substitute cornstarch for tapioca starch as a thickener, or vice versa. Each has its own texture and will affect recipes differently.

 **TIANJIN BOK CHOY** Often called "Tianjin cabbage" or "Tientsin bok choy," the former spelling of its home city, "celery cabbage," or "napa cabbage." It comes in two varieties, one a long stalk type, the other rounder and leafier. It is the latter variety that is most familiar, is the sweeter of the two, and the one I prefer. It is at its best in spring. It may be kept in a plastic bag, refrigerated, for about a week, but just as with bok choy it tends to lose its sweetness. I suggest eating it within 2 days, if not immediately.

 TIANJIN PRESERVED VEGETABLE This mixture of Tianjin bok choy, garlic, and salt, comes either in ceramic crocks from China or in plastic bags from Hong Kong. The labels say "Tianjin preserved vegetable," "Tientsin preserved vegetable," or "Tianjin preserved cabbage." Once opened, the vegetable, in a crock or in a tightly sealed bag and stored in a cool, dry place, will keep for up to a year.

 TIGER LILY BUDS These elongated, dried, reddish brown lily buds are also known to the Chinese as golden needles. The best ones have a softness to them. When dry they become brittle. If they are brittle in the package do not buy them, for they are too old. Placed in a tightly covered jar and stored in a cool, dry place they will keep for at least 6 months.

VINEGARS There are many vinegars used in China, most of them rice based. The aristocrat of Chinese vinegars is Chinkiang vinegar, a thick, black vinegar based on glutinous rice, made along China's northern coast. It has a distinct, direct taste and an aroma that is reminiscent of balsamic vinegar. In recipes you may substitute a commercial balsamic for it, but not an aged balsamic.

Other vinegars, classified as white, are based upon rices or sorghums, or both. They can be labeled "rice vinegar," "grain vinegar," or "white rice vinegar." There are many brands of white vinegars and I find them about equal in taste. For the whites you may substitute a good grain-based distilled white vinegar.

 WATER CHESTNUTS These are not actually nuts. Rather they are bulbs, deep purplish brown in color, that are cultivated in muddy water. Peeling fresh water chestnuts is time consuming, but once they're peeled you'll find them worth the effort. The meat of the water chestnut is white, sweet, juicy, and crisp, and delicious even when eaten raw. Canned water chestnuts are a poor substitute. If you cannot find fresh water chestnuts, I suggest jicama, or *sah gut*. If you keep water chestnuts refrigerated with their skins on, including the mud traces, in a brown paper bag, they will keep for 2 to 3 weeks.

 WHITE RICE WINE I use Chinese white rice wine in many recipes in this book. There are many types and brands with varying strengths, usually referred to as either "double steamed" or "triple steamed." A double steamed white wine is perfect for the recipes in this book, and one that is widely available and very good is Kiu Kiang, or "Nine Mountains" rice wine. If unavailable, a good gin approximates the strength of Chinese white rice wine.

 WINTER MELON This large melon looks like a watermelon and has a similar oblong-round shape. Its skin is dark green, occasionally mottled, while the interior of the fruit is white with a faint green tinge and white seeds. The winter melon has no taste of its own but rather absorbs the flavors of the food it is cooked with. When cooked, usually in soup, or steamed, the melon becomes translucent. You need not buy a whole melon; slices are sold by weight in Chinese and Asian markets.

WRAPPERS The types, sizes, and uses of wrappers, also called skins, in China are endless. So many are available under various names that searching for the right ones for your dumplings or spring rolls can be confusing. What follows is a guide to wrappers.

Won ton wrappers: Also labeled "won ton skins," (occasionally spelled "won tun") these thin wrappers are made from wheat flour, eggs, water, and baking soda. They are about 3 to 3½ inches square, come in plastic packages (about 70 to a package) and can be found in the refrigerated cases at markets. They are also available without eggs.

Dumpling wrappers: These small, pliable wrappers, also labeled as "skins," come 50 to 80 to a plastic-wrapped package, depending on their thickness. They are made from wheat flour and water, with or without salt, with or without eggs, and each is dusted with cornstarch so they will not stick together. They are circular, about 3½ inches in diameter, but can easily be cut with kitchen shears to whatever size you wish. These, too, are to be found in the refrigerated case at the market.

Larger wrappers: There are many types of large wrappers, including "spring roll skins" (or wrappers), "egg roll skins" (or wrappers), and "lumpia wrappers." Usually about 7 inches square, they are usually made from wheat flour, water, and salt, with or without eggs, and are pliable. They come in plastic packages with 10, 12, 20, or 25 wrappers per package, each dusted with cornstarch to prevent sticking. Usually spring roll wrappers are white in color because they have been cooked before packaging. Egg roll skins are usually cream-colored or yellow, and uncooked. Both of these may be used interchangeably.

Other wrappers: "moo shu wrappers," relatively new to the market, are quite thin and elastic and are made specifically for moo shu dishes and Peking duck. They are circular, 8 inches in diameter, and can be found in the refrigerated department of your market. They are convenient and useful, but I prefer the homemade pancakes that are made in a wok (page 161).

Rice paper wrappers: There are two kinds of rice paper, both of which are dried: small circles from Vietnam and Thailand, 6, 7, or 8 inches in diameter, or triangles, 6 inches to a side. They are labeled "rice paper," "rice sheets," and "spring roll skins," but they are made from rice flour, salt, and water. Because these wrappers are dried, they must be immersed in water before use. The other rice paper wrappers are from China, circular, about 9 inches in diameter, extremely soft, and thinner than tissue paper. They come about 75 to a 2.5-ounce plastic package. Labeled "rice paper," the Chinese call them "wafer paper," and they can be used right out of the package. They can also be fried, but must not be moistened, for water makes them disintegrate.

All fresh, refrigerated wrappers should be used quickly. Refrigerated and wrapped in plastic, they will keep for 3 to 4 days. They may be frozen for up to 3 months. To reuse after freezing, allow them to come to room temperature before use. Dry wrappers will keep up to a year, wrapped and stored in a cool, dry place.

A final note on wrappers: there are packs of dried wrappers from Thailand labeled "egg rolls," but they are brittle and essentially unusable.

BASIC RECIPES

In addition to these ingredients I have my own essential preparations that recur in this book as basics, as ingredients, and as flavorings. You will use them over and over again, I am sure.

Chicken Stock

(GAI SEUNG TONG)

I cannot stress too highly the importance of high-quality stock in cooking, particularly in Chinese cooking. I use chicken stock for soups, sauces, and marinades and for blanching and poaching.

3 quarts water plus 7½ quarts cold water

2 whole chickens (8 pounds total), including giblets, fat removed, and each chicken cut into quarters

2 pounds chicken wings

½ pound piece of ginger, cut into thirds, lightly smashed

6 whole garlic cloves, peeled

1 bunch scallions, trimmed and cut into thirds

4 medium onions, quartered

¼ pound fresh coriander, cut into thirds (1 cup)

¼ cup browned onions (page 39)

½ teaspoon white peppercorns

Salt

In a large stockpot, bring the 3 quarts water to a boil. Add the chicken, chicken wings, and giblets and bring back to a boil. Boil for a minute. (This will bring the blood and juices to the top.) Drain the water and run cold water into the pot to rinse the chicken. Drain.

Put the chicken and giblets back into the pot. Add the 7½ quarts cold water and all the remaining ingredients except salt. Cover the pot and bring to a boil over high heat. Add salt to taste and lower the heat to a simmer. Leaving the pot lid slightly ajar, simmer for 4½ hours, skimming off any residue from the surface.

Turn off the heat. Allow to cool for 10 to 15 minutes. Strain and pour the stock into containers and cover. Refrigerated, the stock will keep for 4 to 5 days, or frozen for up to 3 months.

MAKES 5 QUARTS

NOTE: Store-bought prepared stocks are often made without salt. If used immediately, that is satisfactory. However, if stock is made for future use, salt is necessary as a preservative.

Perfect Cooked Rice

(FAN)

We have all heard too often that making properly cooked rice is virtually impossible. This need not be the case. It is easy to make perfect rice, a dish of fluffy, separate grains. Here is a foolproof recipe. I recommend that it be eaten with virtually every recipe in this book, and certainly with stir-fried dishes, a natural pairing. Use extra long-grain rice, either Texas-grown or from Thailand. I prefer so-called "old rice," rice that has been lying about in sacks for extended periods, because it absorbs water more easily and will be easier to cook. The older the rice, the larger the yield.

Put 2 cups rice in a pot with cold water. Wash and drain the rice three times in the pot by rubbing it between your palms. Drain well. Add water to the rice and allow it to rest for an hour before cooking. A good ratio is 2 cups rice to 15 ounces water.

Begin cooking the rice, uncovered by bringing the water to a boil over high heat. Stir the rice with chopsticks or with a wooden spoon, and cook for about 4 minutes or until the water is absorbed or evaporates. Even after the water is gone, the rice will continue to be quite hard. Cover the pot and cook over low heat for about 8 minutes more, stirring the rice from time to time.

Turn off the heat and loosen the rice with chopsticks or a wooden spoon. This will help retain fluffiness. Cover the pot tightly until ready to serve. Just before serving, stir and loosen the rice again. Well-cooked rice will have absorbed the water but will not be lumpy, nor will the kernels stick together; they will be firm and separate. The rice may be kept hot in a warm oven for an hour without drying out.

MAKES 4½ TO 5 CUPS

Infused Oils

(Yau Mei Yau Loi)

Flavored oils have existed in many countries, certainly in China, for centuries. Oils pressed from sesame seeds, turnips, and rapeseed have been used in China for more than two thousand years as the prime source of cooking oil. Peanut oil is most receptive to other flavors and absorbs the scents and flavors of the spices when heated. I suggest using a wok to make these oils because the simple process of heating oil in a wok also seasons it. In this book I recommend using different infusions for different dishes to accent the dishes. You may, of course, simply use peanut oil instead. All of these infusions may be made with soybean, corn, sunflower, or canola oils as well.

Scallion Oil

(Chung Yau)

1½ cups peanut oil
3 to 4 bunches scallions (1 pound),
    trimmed, white portions lightly smashed,
    each scallion cut into 2-inch pieces

Heat a wok over medium heat. Add the peanut oil and then scallions and bring to a boil. Lower the heat and simmer the oil for 20 to 30 minutes, stirring occasionally. When the oil turns golden brown it is done. Turn off the heat and allow to cool in the wok. Strain through a fine strainer into a bowl and cool to room temperature. Pour into a glass jar and refrigerate until needed. The oil will keep at room temperature for a week, or 6 months refrigerated.

Makes 1¼ cups

Note: Do not discard the scallions. They make a tasty addition to soups and stock.

White Peppercorn Oil

(BOK CHIU YAU)

1 cup peanut oil
½ cup white peppercorns

Put the oil and peppercorns in a wok over medium heat and bring to a boil. Reduce the heat to low and cook for 2 minutes. Turn off the heat and allow to cool in the wok. Do not strain; pour the oil and peppercorns in a glass jar and close tightly. Because this oil is so delicate, it will not keep long, so I make only a small amount at a time. It will keep, refrigerated, for up to 2 months.

MAKES 1 SCANT CUP

Onion Oil

(YUNG CHUNG YAU)

1½ cups peanut oil
1 pound yellow onions, very thinly sliced (4 cups)

Heat a wok over high heat for 30 seconds. Add the peanut oil and onions. Stir, making certain the onions are coated. Cook for 7 minutes, stirring and turning often to prevent burning and to ensure even browning. Lower the heat to medium and cook for 15 minutes more or until the onions turn light brown. Turn off the heat. Strain the oil into a bowl, using a ladle or large spoon to press the onions as they drain. Allow to cool. Place in a glass jar and close tightly. The oil will keep at room temperature for a week or refrigerated for up to 6 months.

MAKES 1¼ CUPS

NOTE: The browned onions may be kept indefinitely, refrigerated in a plastic container, for other uses. (I use them in my own chicken stock.)

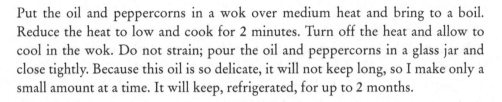

Hot Pepper Oil

(Lot Jiu Yau)

¹/₂ cup hot red pepper flakes
¹/₃ cup sesame oil
¹/₂ cup peanut oil

Place the pepper flakes in a bowl. Bring the oils to a boil and add the pepper flakes. Do not have your face over the bowl because the fumes may cause throat discomfort or coughing. Turn off the heat. After the oil cools, it is ready for use. The pepper flakes should be kept in the oil. They will rest on the bottom and are used in other recipes. Keep in a tightly closed jar at room temperature for a week or refrigerated for 6 months. The longer this oil is stored, the more potent it becomes.

MAKES 1¹/₃ CUPS

Basic Minced Chicken Filling

(Gai Yuk Ham)

In the Chinese kitchen repertoire, many preparations use minced ingredients, either in combination with other foods or as fillings and wrappings. Most of these are fish, shrimp, or pork, and occasionally beef. Rarely is chicken used in this fashion, as chicken was regarded as too valuable and was to be eaten whole, not minced or ground. I have developed the minced filling that follows especially for this book. It is quite like a paste and, as you will see, most versatile.

½ pound chicken cutlets, washed and dried thoroughly with paper towels, cut into ¼-inch dice

3 tablespoons peeled fresh water chestnuts cut into ⅛-inch dice

¼ cup finely sliced scallions

1 tablespoon oyster sauce

1 teaspoon Chinese white rice wine or gin

2 teaspoons sesame oil

½ teaspoon salt

1½ teaspoons sugar

Pinch white pepper

2 tablespoons beaten egg whites

With the blade of a cleaver chop the chicken and dice until a firm paste forms. Put the minced chicken in a bowl, add the remaining ingredients, and mix well with your hands. When well mixed, scoop up the entire mass and slap it against the bottom of the bowl. Repeat nine times. This gives the mass of chicken and spices a cohesiveness that will keep it together no matter how the filling is used.

Alternatively, grind the chicken meat and then place it in the bowl of an electric mixer with all the ingredients except the water chestnuts and scallions. Mix with the flat open paddle blade for 4 minutes, add the water chestnuts and scallions, and mix for 45 seconds more until the ingredients are well blended and cohesive.

I prefer to hand chop the chicken, however, because the filling is firmer and more elastic and I find that the taste is better.

Put the filling in a shallow dish and refrigerate, covered, for 4 hours or overnight before use.

MAKES ½ POUND

Steamed Black Mushrooms

(Gai Yau Dong Gu)

This classic dish is a favorite throughout China and is most versatile. These mushrooms are regarded as foods to serve honored guests at banquets. The mushrooms can be eaten on their own, or as cold or warm appetizers. They can be a side dish, or sliced in combination with other foods. They are an essential dish for this book. The traditional way of preparing them is with chicken fat. You may use oil instead, but the fat is best. It's a good way to use the fat from a fresh chicken.

40 silver dollar-size dried Chinese
  black mushrooms
½ teaspoon salt
2½ teaspoons sugar
1 tablespoon dark soy sauce
2 scallions, trimmed, cut into
  2-inch-long pieces, white
  portions lightly smashed

1 ounce piece raw chicken fat, cut in
  half, or 2 tablespoons peanut oil
1 slice ginger, ½ inch long, lightly
  smashed
1 teaspoon sesame oil
1½ tablespoons Shao-Hsing wine or
  sherry
¼ cup chicken stock (page 36)

Soak the mushrooms in hot water for 30 minutes. Wash thoroughly and squeeze out the excess water. Remove the stems and place the mushrooms in a steamproof dish. Add the other ingredients and toss well. Place the dish in a steamer and steam, covered, for 30 minutes.

Turn off the heat and remove the dish from the steamer. Discard the scallions, ginger, and chicken fat and gently toss the mushrooms in the remaining liquid. Allow the mushrooms to cool to room temperature. Cover with plastic wrap and refrigerate until ready to use. The mushrooms will keep, refrigerated, for 4 to 5 days. They may be frozen with their liquid for at least 5 months. Defrost before use.

The Whole Chicken as Celebration

No feast of any significance in China is complete without a whole chicken as its centerpiece. Because the chicken is symbolic of the phoenix, whole chickens are always served when celebrating the birth of a child. This celebration is held one month after the birth. Birthday celebrations always include chickens, prepared and served in many of the ways that are detailed in this chapter. Engagements and weddings always include chickens, as well.

The Lunar New Year observance, and as a prelude to the obligation to send the kitchen god joyously to Heaven, are marked by serving whole chickens. A word about the kitchen god, whose name is Joh Guan. The paper image of this folkloric god always sat above our kitchen stove. Before the New Year, his mouth was smeared with honey and the image was burned. We believed that the smoke was Joh Guan rising to Heaven where, with his sweetened mouth, he would say only sweet things about our family to the assembled deities.

Whole chickens were offered in Buddhist temples on holidays and festivals. In my family a whole chicken, surrounded by smaller plates of other foods, including three bowls of cooked rice, three bowls of Chinese rice wine, and three pairs of chopsticks, would be placed on an altar. Incense sticks would be lit and we would bow three times, touch the ground with our foreheads three times, and take three steps on our knees toward the altar. This series of threes was an observance that began in imperial China when the emperor was so greeted. After our visit, the chicken and other foods would be taken home for a remembrance feast.

Whole chickens also marked meals held to honor the death dates of ancestors. Each year, usually in March, we observed the Ching Ming festival, when we would visit the gravesites of our ancestors and offer whole chickens to them. On this occasion, we would bring the chickens home after symbolically offering them, and prepare them for dinner. In addition, chickens were always part of a dinner held to observe the recovery of a loved one from illness.

In our family we had whole chickens in a sort of thanksgiving feast. Many of our relatives had migrated away from our town, and even away from China. They would regularly send money to help support elders and those left behind. To give thanks to them we would have feasts of thanksgiving, which we called *sik yeun fan,* or "eat soft rice," indicating that those who had received money were sufficiently well and did not have to work themselves.

The whole chicken was, and is, a symbol of wholeness and of completion.

Virtually all of the recipes that follow are classics, unchanged for many decades, even centuries. What I have done, in most cases, is adapt them to the modern kitchen without destroying their essential historical character. Most important, I have simplified them. To be sure, they are festive dishes and as such may require some effort and time, quite like the amount of time and effort we would put into preparation of our Thanksgiving turkeys.

It is worth repeating that preparing a whole chicken for cooking requires that it be cleaned and rinsed well. I cannot overstate its importance, for the secret to a good and tasty chicken lies in its preparation. This is particularly true for the whole chicken.

Place the whole chicken in a sink and run cold water over it, inside and out. Remove fat and membranes. Run cold water of it again to rid it of residue. (The piece of fat usually found at the rear cavity is perfect for steaming with steamed black mushrooms.) Now rub ¼ cup of salt thoroughly on the outside of the chicken. Rinse it off with cold water. The chicken will be smooth, clean, and without any trace of oily residue. Sit the bird, rear cavity down, in a mesh strainer over a large bowl and allow to drain for an hour.

Beggar's Chicken

(Hot Yee Gai)

叫化鷄

This classic dish originated in Beijing but is claimed by the city of Hangzhou as well. No matter. It is delicious whichever city claims it, though the best versions I have eaten have been in Yangzhou. The name comes from a folk tale about a beggar without a home, money, or food who stole a chicken from a farm and raced off with it. To cook it, because he had no oven, he covered the chicken with mud, made a fire in a hole in the ground, and baked his chicken, peeling off feathers before he ate.

Though commonly known as the chicken of the beggar, it is often called foo guai gai, *or "rich and noble chicken," because it is so rich. Although it is traditionally baked in clay, I use a thick dough, which keeps the chicken moist and its flavors from escaping. It is usually cooked with a strong brown spirit,* Ng Gah Pei, *available in crocks. A good whiskey or brandy will do as well.*

1 whole chicken (3½ pounds), thoroughly cleaned and dried

FOR THE MARINADE
4 tablespoons Ng Gah Pei or whiskey or brandy
1 cinnamon stick, broken into pieces
2 whole eight-star anise, broken into pieces
2 teaspoons salt
1½ tablespoons sugar
Pinch white pepper

FOR THE STUFFING
⅓ cup pieces chicken fat cut into ½-inch dice

1½ cups diced onions
6 dried black mushrooms, washed, soaked in hot water for 20 minutes until softened, stems discarded, caps diced into ½-inch pieces
½ cup preserved vegetable (page 28), washed six times, leaves opened, rinsed thoroughly, squeezed, finely sliced
3 teaspoons Shao-Hsing wine or sherry
1 teaspoon sesame oil
½ teaspoon five-spice seasoning
½ teaspoon salt
2 teaspoons sugar
Pinch white pepper

FOR THE DOUGH
    6 cups all-purpose bleached flour
    2¼ cups hot water, plus
        2 tablespoons, if needed
    2 teaspoons peanut oil

2 lotus leaves, soaked in hot water
    for 20 minutes until softened,
    rinsed, or 1 yard cheesecloth
2 feet heavy-duty foil

Mix all the marinade ingredients and rub the inside and outside of the chicken with it. Set aside.

Prepare the stuffing: Heat a wok over high heat for 30 seconds, add the chicken fat, and cook for 1½ minutes. Add the onions and cook for 2 minutes or until translucent. Add the mushrooms and preserved vegetable, stir, and mix. Add the wine and stir. Add the sesame oil, five-spice seasoning, salt, sugar, and pepper and mix well. Turn off the heat. Remove the stuffing to a bowl and allow to cool.

Prepare the dough: Place the flour on a work surface and make a well in the center. Add the hot water slowly with one hand and mix with the other. When the water is absorbed, knead for about 2 minutes, until a dough is formed. If the dough is hard, add the additional 2 tablespoons of water, one at a time. The dough should have the consistency of bread dough. Coat your hands with peanut oil and rub the dough with pressure to coat it. Rub the work surface as well. Flatten the dough on the work surface until it is large enough to wrap the chicken completely.

Stuff and wrap the chicken: Place the reserved stuffing loosely in the cavity. Close the neck and tail openings by pulling the loose skin to cover. Overlap the lotus leaves. Place the chicken in the center and wrap to cover completely and tightly. (If using cheesecloth, wrap tightly as well.) Place the leaf-wrapped chicken, breast side up, in the center of the flattened dough and wrap the chicken, sealing the edges by pressing firmly with the fingers. Spread out the foil, place the dough-wrapped chicken, breast side up, on top, and fold around the chicken, enclosing it completely.

Preheat the oven to 350° F for 15 minutes. Place the wrapped chicken in a roasting pan, bake for an hour, then lower the heat to 325° F. Bake for 3 more hours. Turn off the heat. Remove the chicken to a platter. Unwrap the foil, cut a large hole in the dough and leaves, and serve by spooning the chicken, stuffing, and juices onto each plate.

MAKES 4 TO 6 SERVINGS

NOTE: The foil insulates the chicken so that it will remain hot enough to serve if removed from the oven an hour prior to serving.

Ching Ping Chicken

(CHING PING GAI)

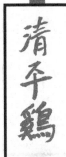

The very famous, very fragrant, Ching Ping market winds through a series of narrow streets and alleys in Guangzhou, known to much of the world as Canton. It is filled with vendors selling fresh vegetables and fruits, live fish and poultry, as well as an enormous variety of dried and preserved foods. On one of my trips to this market, I discovered this recipe as a happy accident. I had stopped to look at racks of cooked and barbecued chickens, ducks, and geese, and was given a taste. "What is this?" I asked the woman shopkeeper. "Ching Ping gai," she answered with a smile. "And how is it made?" I asked. She told me.

8 cups cold water

6 fresh lime leaves (if unavailable, substitute basil)

6 sprigs fresh mint

2 scallions, trimmed and cut in half

2 cinnamon sticks

1 slice ginger, 1 inch long, lightly smashed

¼ cup Shao-Hsing wine or sherry

2 ounces sugarcane sugar, or ¼ cup brown sugar

1½ tablespoons salt

1 whole chicken (3½ pounds) thoroughly cleaned and dried

Place water and all ingredients except chicken in a Dutch oven. Bring to a boil and allow to boil for 5 minutes. Lower the heat. Place the chicken, breast side up, in the liquid. Return to a boil. Reduce the heat, partially cover the pot, and simmer the chicken for 15 minutes. Turn and simmer for an additional 15 minutes. Turn off the heat and allow the chicken to sit in the liquid for 10 minutes more.

Remove the chicken from the liquid and allow to cool to room temperature. Place on a platter, cover with plastic wrap, and refrigerate. When cold, slice and serve.

MAKES 4 TO 6 SERVINGS

NOTE: Ching Ping Chicken will keep, refrigerated, for 3 to 4 days. This recipe has an added bonus. There should be about 8 cups of liquid remaining after cooking the chicken. It is a perfect base for soups. Simply strain and refrigerate, or freeze, as you would with chicken stock.

Chicken Baked in Salt

(Yim Guk Gai)

This may well be the most famous chicken feast in China. It comes from the Hakka people, China's nomads, who began their lives in Mongolia but through centuries of persecution made a forced migration south until they settled in many areas of Guangdong, and particularly in the New Territories of Hong Kong. The salt in this recipe does not make the chicken salty. Rather, it acts like an oven that cooks and seals the chicken.

The Hakka, because they were nomads, had no ovens and no permanent homes, so they would dig a shallow hole in the ground, place stones in it, and create an "oven" out of sea salt. I have simplified this process for the modern kitchen; I use coarse salt in a Dutch oven.

It saddens me to say that you will seldom get genuine Chicken Baked in Salt in restaurants, even if their menus say so. In most cases the chicken is thrust into a series of boiling salt solutions to cook and is presented as salt-baked. It is more satisfying to make your own.

6 pounds kosher salt
1 whole chicken (3½ pounds),
    thoroughly cleaned and dried
2 tablespoons Shao-Hsing wine or
    sherry
3 scallions, trimmed, cut into
    1-inch-long pieces, white
    portions slightly smashed

1 slice ginger, ½ inch long
¼ dried tangerine skin (about
    2 inches long), soaked in hot
    water for 30 minutes until soft
2 lotus leaves, soaked in hot water
    for 20 minutes until soft, rinsed,
    or 4-foot-long piece of
    cheesecloth

Place 3 pounds of the salt in Dutch oven and the remaining 3 pounds in a separate roasting pan and heat at 350° F for 30 minutes, until very hot.

As the salt bakes, prepare the chicken: Rub wine on the outside and inside of the chicken. Place the scallions, ginger, and tangerine skin inside the chicken. Wrap the chicken with overlapping lotus leaves or cheesecloth.

Remove the salt from the oven and raise the oven temperature to 450° F. Make a shallow well in the salt in the Dutch oven. Place the wrapped chicken, breast side up, in the well. Spoon the 3 pounds of salt from the roasting pan over the chicken to cover it completely. Roast, uncovered, for 1 hour and 10 minutes. Turn off the heat. Remove the chicken from the oven and allow to rest for 15 minutes.

Brush away the salt cover and remove the chicken to a platter. Unwrap it and discard the lotus leaves or cheesecloth. Chop the chicken into bite-size pieces and serve with the traditional dip.

Chicken Baked in Salt Dip

4 tablespoons scallion oil (page 38)
4 tablespoons grated ginger
1 teaspoon salt

Combine all the ingredients in a bowl. Spoon into individual small dishes and serve with the chicken.

MAKES 4 TO 6 SERVINGS

Mou Tai Chicken

(JING MOU TAI GAI)

This historic chicken dish, steamed with China's potent distilled spirit Mou Tai, owes its fame to President Richard Nixon's 1972 visit to China. Cooking chicken with Mou Tai—a millet-based spirit that goes back two thousand years to the Han Dynasty—is and was nothing new. But it was considered an unusual dish, and was selected to be cooked for President Nixon as part of the banquet in his honor in the Great Hall of the People of Beijing.

Mou Tai itself was not foreign to the president. He was served glasses of it repeatedly at various diplomatic functions and receptions, usually while Chinese orchestras played "Home on the Range" and "America the Beautiful." The president recalled at one point that in 1972 he had toasted, in Chinese fashion, with Mou Tai, thirty people individually at one dinner, "but I didn't finish the glass. If I had, I wouldn't have lasted."

Henry Kissinger, then secretary of state, who negotiated the Shanghai communique in 1972, said that "late at night after a banquet of Peking duck and powerful Mou Tai liquor," signing and negotiating were easy. Similar banquets were held during Nixon's subsequent visits to China in 1976 and 1982, and the Mou Tai again flowed freely. But it was in 1972 that Mou Tai Chicken was served. Here it is. Eat like a president.

FOR THE MARINADE
- 5 tablespoons Mou Tai
- 2¼ teaspoons salt
- 4½ teaspoons sugar

- 1 whole chicken (3½ pounds), thoroughly cleaned and dried
- 1 slice ginger, ½ inch long, lightly smashed

- 3 scallions, trimmed, cut into 2-inch-long pieces, white portions lightly smashed
- 2-foot-long piece heavy duty foil
- Two 2-foot-long pieces plastic wrap
- 1 lotus leaf, soaked in hot water for 20 minutes until softened, rinsed
- 10 cups boiling water

On a work surface, place the chicken breast side up and loosen the skin with your hands. Turn the chicken over. Using a small knife, loosen the skin from the neck and tail. (All of the skin, including that of the legs, should be loose.)

Combine the marinade ingredients in a bowl. Place the chicken in a shallow dish and drizzle some of the marinade in the cavity, between the skin and the flesh, and all over the outside. Cover the chicken with plastic wrap and allow to marinate for 3 hours in the refrigerator.

Remove the chicken from the refrigerator at least 45 minutes before steaming to allow it to come to room temperature. Place the ginger and scallions in the cavity. Scoop liquid from the dish and drizzle over the chicken and in the cavity. Wrap the chicken by laying the foil flat and laying one length of plastic wrap on top of it, the second across. Lay the lotus leaf in the middle. Place the chicken, breast side up, on the lotus leaf. Wrap tightly. Bring the ends of plastic wrap around the bird, tightly. Bring the foil up and around, folding at the edge to seal. Place the wrapped chicken in a steamer.

Pour the boiling water into a wok. Place the steamer inside, turn the heat to high, and steam for 2½ hours. Every 20 minutes add boiling water to replace that which has evaporated. Turn off the heat. Transfer the chicken from the steamer to a large serving dish.

Partially unwrap the chicken by unfolding the foil and cutting through the plastic wrap and leaf with kitchen shears. This will release the aroma of the Mou Tai. Serve by loosening the meat with a spoon, separating it from the bones, and spooning the sauce over it.

MAKES 4 TO 6 SERVINGS

Mou Tai Chicken II

(Guk Mou Tai Gai)

This is my modern twist on the traditional dish. The preceding recipe is the way it was served to President Nixon but this version is mine. Often people are not quite comfortable steaming an entire chicken; perhaps their cooking equipment is not sufficiently large. So I have adapted the chicken to the baking process. A note: Mou Tai is a strong and pungent spirit. If you wish not to use it, substitute a good, strong gin.

FOR THE MARINADE
  5 tablespoons Mou Tai, or
    6 tablespoons strong gin
  2¼ teaspoons salt
  4½ teaspoons sugar

  1 whole chicken (3½ pounds),
    thoroughly cleaned
    and dried

1 slice ginger, ½ inch long, lightly
  smashed
3 scallions, trimmed, cut into
  2-inch-long pieces, white
  portions lightly smashed
2 lotus leaves, soaked in hot water
  for 20 minutes until softened,
  rinsed
2-foot-long piece heavy duty foil

Follow the instructions of the first three paragraphs in the preceding recipe, except wrap the chicken in this manner: Place the lotus leaves on a flat countertop, one overlapping the other. Place the chicken on the leaves and wrap tightly. Cover with foil and seal by folding at the edges. Place the wrapped chicken in a roasting pan.

Preheat the oven to 450° F for 20 minutes. Place the chicken in the oven and bake for 30 minutes. Lower the heat to 400° F and bake for an hour more. Lower the heat to 325° F and bake for another hour. (During this last phase the aroma of the Mou Tai will become evident.)

Turn off the heat. Remove the chicken to a serving platter, unwrap the foil, and cut a large hole in the lotus leaves. Serve with a spoon as in the preceding recipe.

MAKES 4 TO 6 SERVINGS

Cantonese Fried Chicken

(Jah Ji Gai)

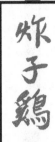

This is a banquet dish that has been part of my life since I was young. In Canton there is a very famous restaurant, Bun Kai, also called Pan Xi, that has been in business for many decades. I remember being taken there by my aunts, and it was there that I first ate Jah Ji Gai. On a recent visit to Canton I went to the restaurant, now the province of one of China's most famed chefs, Fan Hawn Hung. He shared with me his recipe for this fried chicken. In recent years it has also acquired the name of "Peking chicken," but it is southern, not northern. I have modified Chef Fan's recipe slightly to suit the Western kitchen.

1 whole chicken (3½ pounds), cleaned thoroughly and dried

¼ cup Chinese white rice wine or gin

1 whole nutmeg

FOR THE POACHING

3 whole eight-star anise

¼ dried tangerine skin (about 2 inches long)

3 cinnamon sticks

1 slice ginger, 1 inch long, lightly smashed

10 cups cold water

2 tablespoons salt

2 tablespoons sugar

FOR THE COATING

1½ tablespoons honey melted with 3 tablespoons boiling water

1½ teaspoons Shao-Hsing wine or sherry

1½ teaspoons Chinese white rice vinegar

¾ teaspoon cornstarch

6 cups peanut oil

Combine the poaching ingredients in a large pot (preferably an oval Dutch oven) and bring to a boil. Cover the pot, lower the heat, and simmer for 20 minutes. Raise the heat to high and return to a boil. Place the chicken in the pot, breast side up. Cover. When the pot begins to boil, lower the heat and simmer for 15 minutes. Turn the chicken over and repeat the process.

Turn off the heat and allow the chicken to sit in the liquid, covered, for 10 minutes. Remove the chicken to a rack that has been set into a platter and allow to drain. Pierce the skin with a fork to help the draining. Discard all the ingredients from the pot. Reserve poaching liquid for later use.

(continued)

Mix the coating ingredients, and with a pastry brush, coat the chicken thoroughly with the mixture. Allow the chicken to dry completely, about 6 hours. During this time, turn the chicken, taking care not to mar the coating. (An electric fan can reduce the drying time by half.)

Heat a wok over high heat for a minute. Add the peanut oil and heat it to 375° F. Using a large Chinese strainer, lower the chicken into the oil, breast side up, and deep-fry for 3 minutes. Use a ladle to pour oil over the chicken to ensure uniformity in frying. Turn the chicken over by inserting a wooden spoon in its cavity, and deep-fry for another 3 minutes, ladling the oil as before. Repeat until the chicken is golden brown. Turn off the heat. Remove the chicken and allow it to drain. Place the chicken on a chopping board, cut into bite-size pieces, and serve immediately with the roasted spice salt.

Roasted Spice Salt

2 teaspoons salt
$\frac{1}{2}$ teaspoon five-spice seasoning
$\frac{1}{2}$ teaspoon Sichuan peppercorns

Heat a wok over high heat for 45 seconds. Lower the heat and add all the ingredients to the wok. Dry-roast (see page 16), stirring, until the five-spice seasoning turns black. Turn off the heat. Strain off the peppercorns and discard them. Place the roasted spice salt in individual small dishes and serve with the chicken.

MAKES 4 TO 6 SERVINGS

White Cut Chicken

(Bok Chi Gai)

This festive chicken is as popular in Hong Kong as coq au vin is in France. It is white cut chicken that is brought most often as a temple offering, and the chicken is eaten on the day of the kitchen god, Joh Guan, to remember relatives who have left China, particularly those who traveled to California and the "Golden Mountain" of San Francisco. Each May in Hong Kong there are dragon boat races, with brightly decorated boats representing cities, provinces, towns, and villages of China. Each boat carries a team of synchronized rowers, who compete for prizes. Before the races, white cut chicken is offered by each boat to the gods as a prayer for success and to ask that there be no injuries.

10 cups water	3 tablespoons sugar
3 scallions, trimmed and cut in half	1 whole chicken (3½ pounds), cleaned thoroughly and dried
2 tablespoons salt	

Put the water, scallions, salt, and sugar in a large pot (preferably a Dutch oven) and bring to a boil. Place the chicken in the pot, breast side up, and cover. Return to a boil and then lower the heat and simmer for 15 minutes. Turn the chicken over, cover the pot, and simmer for another 15 minutes. Turn off the heat. Allow the chicken to rest in the pot, covered, for another 30 minutes.

Remove the chicken from the pot and drain well, making certain there is no water in the cavity. Place the chicken on a chopping board and cut into bite-size pieces. Serve at room temperature with the ginger soy dipping sauce (recipe follows).

MAKES 4 TO 6 SERVINGS

(continued)

Ginger Soy Dipping Sauce

1 tablespoon dark soy sauce
1 tablespoon light soy sauce
2 tablespoons chicken stock (page 36)
1 tablespoon minced ginger
2 tablespoons minced scallions, white part only
2 teaspoons sesame oil
1 teaspoon sugar

Mix all ingredients in a bowl, spoon into individual small dishes, and serve with the chicken.

MAKES 4 TO 6 SMALL SERVINGS

Cinnamon-Scented Chicken

(Heung So Gai)

I love this recipe for two reasons. First, it illustrates an often overlooked aspect of the Sichuan table. In general, it is thought that the cooking of Sichuan is all heat and spice, but it can be delicate and elegant as well, which is proven in this traditional dish. Second, it provides an added bonus. If chopped fresh vegetables are added to the cooking liquid, a flavorful soup emerges as a first or second course.

1 whole chicken (3½ pounds), cleaned thoroughly and dried
5 cups cold water
1 cup Shao-Hsing wine or sherry
1 slice ginger, 1 inch long, lightly smashed
3 whole eight-star anise
¼ teaspoon Sichuan peppercorns
2 cinnamon sticks

¼ dried tangerine skin (about 2 inches long)
2 scallions, trimmed and cut in half
3 teaspoons salt
3½ teaspoons sugar
1 tablespoon dark soy sauce
1 egg, beaten
⅓ cup tapioca starch, or enough to coat chicken
6 cups peanut oil

Place the chicken breast side up in a large oval Dutch oven. Add the water, wine, ginger, star anise, peppercorns, cinnamon sticks, tangerine skin, scallions, salt, and sugar, cover the pot, and bring to a boil. Add the dark soy sauce, cover the pot, lower the heat, and simmer for 20 minutes. Turn the chicken over and simmer for another 20 minutes. Turn off the heat. Remove the chicken to a rack set into a platter and allow to dry for 4 to 5 hours.

Place the chicken in a dish and coat with the beaten egg. Spread the tapioca starch on a piece of waxed paper and coat the chicken thoroughly by rolling it in the starch.

Heat a wok over high heat for 30 seconds. Add the peanut oil and heat to 375° F. Place the chicken in a large Chinese strainer and lower it into the oil. Deep-fry for 5 to 7 minutes until golden brown. Ladle the oil over the chicken as it fries to ensure even cooking. Turn off the heat, remove to a cutting board, and cut the chicken into bite-size pieces and serve.

Makes 4 to 6 servings

THE WHOLE CHICKEN AS CELEBRATION

Soy Sauce Chicken

(See Yau Gai)

This unusual and festive chicken was always prepared for the birthday of my grandmother, Ah Paw. It was always a dish of honor, a kind of homage to her as matriarch. And, of course, we loved eating it, too. This recipe provides what is often called a lo soi, or "mother sauce." Once made, it can be used to cook chicken again and again, indefinitely, should you wish. Each time it is used, additional seasonings are added. The older the sauce gets, the better it tastes. In restaurants "mother sauces" are never discarded, and chefs have even been known to carry their sauces with them to other positions.

6 cups chicken stock (page 36)
3 cinnamon sticks
4 whole eight-star anise
1 slice ginger, 2 inches long, lightly smashed

4 ounces sugarcane sugar, or ½ cup brown sugar
1 cup mushroom soy sauce
1 cup Shao-Hsing wine or sherry
1 whole chicken (3½ pounds), cleaned thoroughly and dried

Put the chicken stock, cinnamon, star anise, ginger, and sugar in a large pot and bring to a boil over high heat. Add the mushroom soy and return to a boil. Lower the heat and allow the sauce to simmer for 20 minutes. Return the heat to high, add the wine and return to a boil. Lower the chicken, breast side up, into the liquid and return to a boil. Lower the heat, cover, and simmer for 20 minutes. Turn the chicken over and simmer for another 20 minutes. Turn off the heat and allow the chicken to rest in the liquid, covered, for an hour.

Transfer the chicken to a cutting board. Cut into bite-sized pieces and serve.

MAKES 4 TO 6 SERVINGS

These two remaining festive chicken recipes are unique. They can of course be eaten, as prepared, roasted or poached, but just as often they are cooked to provide chicken meat for other recipes. Many of these are included in other chapters.

Traditionally, chickens were almost never roasted in the Chinese home, simply because most people did not have ovens. Roasting was done in the brick ovens of restaurants and shops that specialized in barbecued and roasted birds. Only later, with the advent of ovens, did Chinese food in the home move from the stovetop, and home roasting and baking was quickly adopted. These days roasted chickens abound in all regions of China. I became more knowledgeable about roasting chickens when I moved to Hong Kong, but I became a devotee after learning how to roast under the tutelage of my mother-in-law when I came to the United States. I quickly added my own variations to the art and these days when I roast a chicken its flavors are distinctly Chinese.

Poached chickens, on the other hand, were always cooked in the home, and usually with an aromatic vegetable. Chickens were poached with coriander, onions, scallions, or carrots, but most often with Chinese celery. This celery is quite different from the stalks found in the United States. Its bright green stalks are very thin, almost like chopsticks, and the leaves are like Western celery. Chinese celery is sweeter than American celery with a more defined aroma, whether raw or cooked. Chinese refer to it as heung kon, or "fragrant celery." When it is cooked, particularly when poached, it releases a pleasant aroma that permeates the chicken. If you cannot obtain Chinese celery, you may use Western celery, but its aroma will be less intense.

Roasted Chicken

(Guk Gai)

1 large whole chicken (6½ pounds),
    such as an oven roaster, cleaned
    thoroughly and dried
2 tablespoons Chinese white rice
    vinegar or distilled vinegar
4 tablespoons Shao-Hsing wine or
    sherry
2½ teaspoons salt

¼ teaspoon white pepper
6 garlic cloves, thinly sliced
1 slice ginger, ½ inch long, lightly
    smashed
2 scallions, trimmed, cut into
    quarters, white portions lightly
    smashed
1 cup water

Preheat the oven to 450° F.

Place the chicken in a roasting pan, and rub all over with rice vinegar and then with the wine. Sprinkle with salt, then with white pepper. Place 2 slices of garlic cloves on the chicken at random, between the skin and the meat. Place the ginger, scallions, and slices of 2 more garlic cloves in the chicken cavity. Place the chicken on a rack in a roasting pan, breast side up, and dot with slices of another garlic clove. Add the water to the roasting pan.

Place the chicken in the oven and roast for 10 minutes. Lower the temperature to 375° F and roast for 30 minutes. Remove the chicken from the oven, turn over, and dot with the remaining garlic slices. With a fork, pierce the skin all over. Place the chicken back in the oven and roast for 30 minutes. Turn the chicken over again so the breast is facing up, and pierce the skin to ensure that the fat runs off. Lower the temperature to 350° F and roast for 30 to 40 minutes more. Turn off the heat. Remove from the oven. Allow to rest for 10 minutes before serving.

MAKES UP TO 8 SERVINGS

Chicken Poached with Chinese Celery

(Heung Kon Bo Gai)

3½ quarts cold water

3 heads Chinese celery, cut into
    2-inch-long pieces (2 cups), leaves
    retained, or 4 stalks Western celery

2½ cups fresh coriander cut into
    3-inch-long pieces

12 whole shallots, peeled

1 slice ginger, 3 inches long, lightly
    smashed

8 scallions, trimmed and cut into
    2-inch-long lengths

1½ tablespoons salt

1 large whole chicken (6½ pounds),
    such as an oven roaster, including
    neck and giblets, cleaned
    thoroughly and dried

½ cup Shao-Hsing wine or sherry

FOR THE DIPPING SAUCE

3 tablespoons light soy sauce

3 tablespoons mushroom
    soy sauce

3 teaspoons Chinese white rice wine
    vinegar or distilled vinegar

2 teaspoons sesame oil

3 teaspoons minced ginger

3 teaspoons minced garlic

⅓ cup finely sliced scallions

1 tablespoon sugar

⅛ teaspoon white pepper

½ cup poaching liquid

Combine the water, celery, coriander, shallots, ginger, scallions, salt, neck, and giblets in a large pot. Cover the pot and bring to a boil over high heat. Lower the heat and simmer for 20 minutes. Turn the heat back to high and add the wine. Turn off the heat. Place the chicken in the pot, breast side up. Return the heat to high and return to a boil. Lower the heat, cover the pot, and simmer for 25 minutes. Turn the chicken over and simmer for another 20 minutes. Turn off the heat and allow the chicken to rest in the liquid, covered, for 20 minutes.

As the chicken rests, combine the dipping sauce ingredients with the poaching liquid from the pot.

Remove the chicken from the pot. The neck and giblets may be set aside for eating or for another use. Remove and discard the skin. Cut the chicken into bite-size pieces, place on a platter, and serve with small individual dishes of dipping sauce.

MAKES UP TO 8 SERVINGS

(continued)

THE WHOLE CHICKEN AS CELEBRATION

NOTES: Strain off the poaching liquid for future use. It can be eaten as a soup as is, or you can add vegetables. It can be refrigerated for 3 days or frozen for up to 2 months.

The meat from both roasted and poached chickens can be kept refrigerated for 3 days or frozen for up to 2 months. Defrost before use.

Chicken as First Course

SMALL DISHES AND APPETIZERS

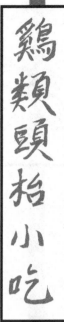

*I*n Shanghai virtually every meal is prefaced by a series of small dishes and appetizers. These serve not only to satisfy hunger and accompany welcoming sips of wine, spirits, or beer, but to whet the appetite for what is to follow.

This custom exists in varying degrees throughout China, but in Shanghai it is a treasured tradition. I have been treated to as many as fifteen of these small tastes before a meal, more courses than in the meal itself, and in any Shanghai restaurant a menu will list as many as fifty or sixty of these dishes.

These small dishes range from cooked to raw, hot to cold, and preserved to fresh, and include such dishes as Shanghai's famed drunken chicken, boiled and fried nuts, crisp fried seaweed, and lima beans or so-called "hairy" soy beans cooked with the preserved green called red in snow. From hot and spicy cabbage to smoked fish and preserved turnips, from crisply fried eel to tiny cooked shrimp, the variety is truly endless, and the concept has influenced restaurant tables throughout China.

In this chapter you will find a selection of these small dishes, all of them using chicken and all of them easily made in advance. Some recipes are traditional, some are new, and some are my adaptations of traditional dishes. I have added chicken to original recipes and I have substituted chicken for different proteins.

I am certain that you will do as I have often done and make a meal of many courses from these small dishes.

Hacked Chicken

(Pong Pong Gai)

This dish, simple to make, attractive to the eye, and delicious, is known throughout China and is a familiar entry on restaurant menus. Traditionally it was made with crushed fah sung, *or ground nuts, which is what the Chinese call peanuts. But peanut butter works very well indeed; it blends well and is very convenient. What household does not have peanut butter?*

Two 1-pound whole chicken
    breasts, with bones and skin
    intact, cleaned thoroughly
    and dried
6 cups water
4 scallions, trimmed and cut in half
1 teaspoon salt
2 teaspoons sugar
1 slice ginger, ¼ inch long, lightly
    smashed
2 whole garlic cloves, peeled
1½ cups shredded iceberg
    lettuce

FOR THE SAUCE
5½ tablespoons liquid from boiling
    chicken
2½ tablespoons peanut butter
2½ tablespoons dark soy sauce
2½ teaspoons sugar
4½ teaspoons Chinkiang vinegar or
    balsamic vinegar
2½ teaspoons minced garlic
1½ teaspoons minced ginger
2½ teaspoons hot pepper oil
    (page 40)
5 teaspoons sesame oil
1½ teaspoons Shao-Hsing wine or
    sherry
4½ tablespoons finely sliced
    scallions

Place the chicken breasts in a large pot. Add the water, scallions, salt, sugar, ginger, and garlic. Cover and bring to a boil over high heat. Lower the heat, partially cover, and cook for 20 minutes. Halfway through the cooking time, turn the breasts over. Turn off the heat and allow the chicken to rest in the liquid for 15 minutes. Remove from the pot and place the chicken in the refrigerator to cool for 3 hours.

Make the sauce: As soon as you have turned off the heat, remove the 5½ table-spoons of the hot cooking liquid to a bowl and combine it with the peanut butter (the hot liquid will liquefy the peanut butter). Add the remaining sauce ingredients and mix well. Reserve the sauce.

Remove the chicken from the refrigerator. Remove the skin and fat and break the breasts in half. Remove any bones. Place the chicken on a chopping board and beat it with a rolling pin or wooden dowel. Tear the breast meat into shreds with your fingers. Toss the chicken with the reserved sauce and coat it well. Spread the shredded lettuce on a platter, mound the shredded chicken on top, and serve.

MAKES 4 SERVINGS

Two-Sesame Chicken

(Ji Mah Gai See)

Black or white sesame seeds are very special in China. The fine, scented oil from pressed sesame seeds imparts fragrance to cooked dishes, and the seeds themselves are fragrant, particularly after they have been roasted. Sprinkled on dishes they add a nutty aroma, as in this delicious dish that I have created.

FOR THE SAUCE
  1 tablespoon light soy sauce
  2½ teaspoons Chinese white rice
    wine vinegar or distilled vinegar
  1 teaspoon Shao-Hsing wine or
    sherry
  2 teaspoons sesame oil
  2 teaspoons sugar
  1 tablespoon chicken stock
    (page 36)

¼ teaspoon salt
Pinch white pepper

2 cups poached chicken meat cut
  into pieces 2 inches by ¼ inch
  along the grain
2 tablespoons finely sliced scallions
1¾ teaspoons white sesame seeds
1¾ teaspoons black sesame seeds
2 cups shredded iceberg lettuce

Mix the sauce ingredients in a bowl. Add the chicken and toss well to combine. Add the sliced scallions, mix well again, and reserve.

Put both the white and black sesame seeds in a wok and dry-roast them (see page 16) for 2 minutes, until their aroma is released and the white sesame seeds turn light brown. Allow to cool.

Spread shredded lettuce on a serving platter. Mound the chicken with sauce on top, sprinkle with sesame seeds, and serve.

MAKES 4 SERVINGS

*T*he following two preparations are examples of serving chicken with the tropi-cal fruits and many vegetables available in southern China in Guangdong province.

Chicken and Melon Salad

(Mot Gua Gai Sah Lut)

Melons are some of Asia's food treasures. Where I grew up in Sun Tak, in southern China, we had unlimited melons. We ate them fresh and sweet; we pickled their rinds when they were green and unripe; we cooked them; we dried them for snacks. One melon in particular, the Hami, is unique to China. It is quite like can-taloupe but crisper and sweeter. This salad, made with cantaloupe, evokes memo-ries of my childhood. You may use honeydew or other similar melon, but whichever you use, it must be firm and ripe.

FOR THE SAUCE
  1½ tablespoons red wine vinegar
  1½ tablespoons sugar
  1 tablespoon light soy sauce
  1 teaspoon Shao-Hsing wine or
    sherry
  2 teaspoons sesame oil
  ¾ teaspoon salt
  ⅛ teaspoon white pepper

1 cup poached chicken meat cut
  into 2½-inch-long julienne
1⅓ cups firm but ripe cantaloupe
  cut into 2½-inch-long julienne
1 medium red bell pepper, julienne
  (¾ cup)
1 celery stalk, cut into 2-inch-long
  julienne (¾ cup)
3 fresh water chestnuts, peeled and
  julienned (¼ cup)
2 scallions, white portions halved
  and julienned (¼ cup)

Mix the sauce ingredients in a bowl. Add the chicken and the remaining ingredi-ents and toss to combine well. Transfer to a platter and serve.

MAKES 4 SERVINGS

CHICKEN AS FIRST COURSE

Spicy Chicken Salad with Jicama and Carrots

(Gai See Sah Lut)

This is another use for poached chicken. What makes it particularly good for cool salads is the lingering taste of the poaching liquid, which is intensified in the chicken through refrigeration. This is another cooling salad, a dish for warm days, and I have deliberately substituted jicama, or sah gut, *for the water chestnuts that would usually be used to demonstrate how crisp the jicama is and how well it substitutes for the water chestnuts. This salad is best served cold.*

FOR THE SAUCE
1½ tablespoons Chinese white rice
   wine vinegar or distilled vinegar
1½ tablespoons sugar
¾ to 1 teaspoon hot pepper oil
   (page 40)
¾ teaspoon salt
2 teaspoons light soy sauce
1 tablespoon Shao-Hsing wine or
   sherry
Pinch white pepper

1¼ cups poached chicken meat
   shredded by hand into 2-inch
   lengths
1¼ cups jicama cut into 2-inch-long
   julienne
¾ cup carrots cut into 2-inch-long
   julienne
¼ cup white parts scallions
   shredded into 2-inch lengths

Put the sauce ingredients in a bowl and mix well. Be sure that the sugar and salt are dissolved. Add the chicken, jicama, carrots, and scallions and toss well to combine. Refrigerate for 2 hours before serving.

MAKES 4 SERVINGS

Drunken Chicken

(Joi Gai)

This is a famous Shanghai preparation, one that is included in virtually every important banquet. The chicken is called "drunken" (joi) because it is flavored with wine. It is offered as both part of a banquet or as one of the small appetizers before a meal. It is usually made with a whole chicken, steamed or poached, then cut up and marinated in a wine-based sauce. I have simplified it by using chicken breasts, with no noticeable difference in flavor. The Chinese name for drunkeness is joi, perhaps apt.

Strain the boiling liquid and reserve for another use. It is a fine base for a soup if you add vegetables.

8 cups cold water
2 large chicken breasts (3 pounds),
  skin and bones intact, cleaned
  thoroughly and dried
2 scallions, trimmed and cut in half
⅓ cup fresh coriander leaves and
  stems cut into 3-inch-long pieces
2 onions, cut into quarters
1 slice ginger, 1 inch long, lightly
  smashed

1 tablespoon salt
2 tablespoons sugar

For the wine sauce
5 tablespoons liquid from boiling
  chicken
4 tablespoons Shao-Hsing wine or
  sherry
1 teaspoon salt
2 teaspoons sugar
Pinch white pepper

Combine the water, chicken breasts, scallions, coriander, onions, ginger, salt, and sugar in a large pot. Cover the pot and bring to a boil over high heat. Lower the heat and simmer for 30 minutes. Turn off the heat and allow the chicken to rest in liquid, covered, for 15 minutes.

While the chicken rests, make the wine sauce. In a bowl, combine the boiling liquid, wine, salt, sugar, and pepper. Reserve.

Remove the chicken from the pot and allow to cool. Remove the skin and bones and cut the chicken meat into 1-inch-long by 2-inch-wide slices. Place in a shallow serving dish. Stir the reserved sauce and pour it over the chicken. Refrigerate for 2 hours, covered. Serve cold.

MAKES 4 TO 6 SERVINGS

CHICKEN AS FIRST COURSE

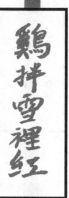

Chicken with Red in Snow and Lima Beans

(Gai Bun Seut Loi Hung)

This, too, is a Shanghai tradition, combining that wonderful preserved green, red in snow, with cooked beans. The beans can vary from so-called "hairy" soybeans to broad favas or limas. I use limas because I find them compatible with the greens and poached chicken. Adding chicken to this Shanghai dish is a fresh take on an old classic. This can be eaten as an appetizer and I have even served it as part of a buffet of many dishes.

½ pound fresh or frozen baby lima
   beans
2½ cups cold water
1 tablespoon scallion oil (page 38)
1 slice ginger, 1½ inches long,
   lightly smashed

2 whole garlic cloves, peeled and
   lightly smashed
½ teaspoon salt
1 cup poached chicken meat cut into
   ½-inch dice
⅔ cup red in snow (see page 28)

Put the fresh beans and water in a large pot and bring to a boil over high heat. Lower the heat to medium and cook for 10 to 12 minutes, or until tender. Run cold water into the pot and drain. (For frozen limas, defrost at room temperature and place them in the boiling water for 20 to 30 seconds. Turn off the heat. Run cold water into the pot, and drain.)

Heat a wok over high heat for 30 seconds. Add the oil and coat the wok with it, using a spatula. Add the ginger, garlic, and salt and stir. When the garlic turns light brown, add the chicken. Stir and mix well for a minute. Add the lima beans and red in snow, stir well, and cook for 2 minutes. Turn off the heat. Transfer to a heated dish and serve.

Makes 4 servings

Shredded Chicken with Mustard Sauce

(Gai Lot Gai See)

This dish is from a small district in Guangdong province, close to Canton. Originally the dish was made with chicken flavored with crushed mustard seeds, then with prepared mustard, and still later—when the dish was prepared in Guangzhou (Canton)—with the prepared hot mustard powder brought to China by the English. These days it is difficult to find in restaurants but is quite simple to make at home.

1 pound chicken cutlets, thoroughly cleaned and dried

FOR STEAMING
1½ teaspoons light soy sauce
1½ tablespoons Shao-Hsing wine or sherry
1½ teaspoons sugar
1½ teaspoons peanut oil
3 scallions, trimmed and cut into 2-inch-long pieces
1 slice ginger, ½ inch long, lightly smashed

FOR THE DRESSING
1 tablespoon sesame paste

2 tablespoons minced shallots
½ teaspoon salt
2¼ teaspoons sugar
4 tablespoons hot liquid from steaming
1½ tablespoons oyster sauce
1½ teaspoons onion oil (page 39)
1½ teaspoons dark soy sauce
1½ tablespoons Shao-Hsing wine or sherry
4 teaspoons Coleman's dry mustard mixed with 4 teaspoons liquid from steaming

Red lettuce or frisee for garnish

Place the chicken in a steamproof dish. Add the steaming ingredients and coat the chicken well. Steam for 20 minutes or until cooked. Turn off the heat. Remove the chicken and allow to cool. Reserve the liquid that remains in the dish.

Make the dressing: Put the sesame paste, shallots, salt, and sugar in a bowl. Add the 4 tablespoons hot steaming liquid and mix well until the sesame paste dissolves. Add the oyster sauce, oil, soy sauce, wine, and mustard and combine until well blended.

Hand shred the chicken into ½-inch lengths and add it to the dressing. Mix thoroughly, making certain the chicken is well coated. Spread red lettuce leaves on a platter, mound the dressed chicken on it, and serve at room temperature.

MAKES 4 SERVINGS

Red Oil Chicken Ding

(Hung Yau Gai Ding)

This unusual dish has its roots in Sichuan. The Sichuan love of heat is evident in the use of hot oil, that peculiar Sichuan peppercorn paste, and in the fact that neither of these ingredients—while they flavor intensely—is used in the cooking process but flavors the chicken after it has been poached. As with many others, this dish can be a first or a main course. The beauty of this traditional preparation lies in its final assembly. Eyes widen when the rice noodles are deep-fried. It makes a beautiful showpiece.

4 cups water

1 slice ginger, ½ inch long, lightly smashed

2 scallions, trimmed and cut into thirds

½ teaspoon salt

1 tablespoon sugar

¾ pound chicken cutlets, cleaned thoroughly and dried

½ cup raw peanuts

FOR THE SAUCE

2½ tablespoons sesame paste

1 tablespoon light soy sauce

3 tablespoons finely sliced scallions

2½ teaspoons sugar

1½ teaspoons hot pepper oil (page 40)

1 teaspoon minced garlic

3½ teaspoons Sichuan peppercorn paste (page 30)

1½ tablespoons Shao-Hsing wine or sherry

½ teaspoon salt

1 tablespoon Chinkiang vinegar or balsamic vinegar

2 ounces dried rice noodles

8 cups peanut oil

1½ cups shredded iceberg lettuce

Poach the chicken: Put the water, ginger, scallions, salt, and sugar in a pot. Cover and bring to a boil over high heat. Add the chicken and allow to return to a boil. Lower the heat and simmer for 15 minutes or until the chicken is cooked through. Turn off the heat. Transfer the chicken to a cutting board, cut into ½-inch dice, and place in a bowl.

While the chicken poaches, dry-roast the peanuts (see page 16). Reserve.

Make the sauce: In a small bowl, mash the sesame paste and then add the remaining sauce ingredients. Mix well. Pour the sauce over the chicken and mix well. Set aside.

Cook the rice noodles: Heat a wok over high heat for a minute, add the peanut oil, and heat to 350° F. With your fingers, loosen the noodles and place in a Chinese strainer. Lower the strainer into the oil very briefly, no more than 1 to 2 seconds. The rice noodles will expand to about ten times their bulk in that time and turn snowy white. Pull the strainer out of the oil, turn off the heat, and allow the rice noodles to drain over a bowl.

Assemble the dish: Spread the shredded lettuce over a platter. Spread the fried rice noodles over the lettuce. Add the dry-roasted nuts to the chicken and sauce and mix well. Mound the chicken atop the fried noodles. Serve immediately at room temperature.

MAKES 4 SERVINGS

NOTE: The dry-roasted peanuts may be prepared in advance. I do not recommend the same for the rice noodles; they are quite fragile and become soggy very quickly.

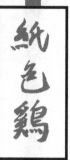

Wafer-Wrapped Chicken Rolls

(Jee Bau Gai)

It may be a surprise to some to learn that China has its own rice paper to enfold foods, quite like those of Southeast Asia. When I was growing up we ate deep-fried rolls filled with chicken and other ingredients, very different from the more familiar spring rolls. These special treats were always enjoyed in restaurants and food shops rather than in the home.

Chinese rice paper wrappers, most of which come from Guangdong province, are quite fragile. A 2.5-ounce package, usually labeled "rice paper," holds about seventy-five "wafers," 9 inches in diameter. A delicate touch is necessary when using them. Unlike the customary rice paper wrappers, they are used right out of the package, without having to be softened. They fry quickly and because they are almost transparent, their fillings can be seen.

24 slices poached chicken about
    1 inch wide by 1½ inches long by
    ⅛ inch thick
1½ teaspoons sesame oil
⅛ teaspoon salt
½ teaspoon sugar
12 Chinese round rice paper
    wrappers

3 steamed black mushrooms
    (page 42), squeezed dry of liquid
    and finely sliced (their length
    should match that of a chicken
    slice)
2 scallions, white parts shredded
    into 1½-inch lengths
6 cups peanut oil

Place the chicken slices in a shallow dish and toss gently with the sesame oil, salt, and sugar to coat. Allow to rest for 10 minutes.

Make the chicken rolls: Lay out a round of rice paper on a dry dinner plate. At one end, about 2 inches in from the edge, place a slice of chicken. On top of this place 3 slices of mushroom, then 4 or 5 shreds of scallion. Top this with another slice of chicken to create a sandwich. Roll tightly, bringing the edges of the rice paper against the chicken. Continue to roll until the wrapper has been rolled about three-quarters of the way, then fold the sides in and around the chicken. Fold in the end of the round and moisten with water to seal. This creates a pillow-like roll. Repeat until all 12 rolls are made.

Heat a wok over high heat for a minute. Add the peanut oil and heat the oil to

350° F. Slide 6 of the chicken rolls into the oil and deep-fry for about 2½ minutes, turning the rolls frequently so they will fry evenly. They will not brown, nor will they become crisp. They remain pale and soft, which is how they should be. Remove from the oil with a strainer or a slotted spoon and drain on paper towels. Repeat with the remaining 6 rolls. Turn off the heat. Serve immediately.

MAKES 4 TO 6 SERVINGS

Rice Paper Chicken Rolls

(Mai Jee Gai See Gun)

These Vietnamese- and Thai-style rolls are more traditional, more familiar rice paper rolls, but I have adapted them to my own taste. Rice paper is an ideal wrapper for fresh, raw vegetables and for the poached chicken with which I combine them. These hard and brittle wrappers from Southeast Asia must be moistened until they become pliable.

FOR THE SAUCE
2 tablespoons Chinese white rice
   vinegar or distilled vinegar
3 tablespoons light soy sauce
3 teaspoons sugar
3½ tablespoons chicken stock
   (page 36)
2 teaspoons sesame oil
1 tablespoon minced red chilies,
   with seeds
2 teaspoons minced garlic

1¼ cups poached chicken meat
   shredded into 2½-inch lengths
½ cup shredded carrots
¾ cup julienned jicama
1 cup fresh bean sprouts, washed and
   drained, green skins discarded
24 sprigs fresh coriander (if
   unavailable, substitute fresh mint
   or Thai basil)
24 rice paper wrappers (6 inches in
   diameter)

Mix the sauce ingredients in a bowl. Reserve.

On a large platter arrange mounds of chicken, carrots, jicama, bean sprouts, and coriander. Cover with plastic wrap and refrigerate for 2 hours until cool but not cold.

Make and serve the rice paper rolls: Remove the filling from the refrigerator and set it in the middle of the table, with a bowl of the sauce on the side. Wet each round of rice paper by passing it through a shallow dish of water and then stack the papers on a plate. (They will soften as they absorb the water but will not stick together, and you will be able to remove each pliable wrapper individually.) To eat, place a wrapper on your plate and mound items from the platter on the wrapper. Spoon a bit of the sauce on top. Then roll the wrapper tightly around the mixture, fold in the ends, and roll into a cigar-like bundle. This finger food is now ready to eat. Serve with fingerbowls.

MAKES FROM 4 TO 8 SERVINGS, DEPENDING ON COURSE

Diced Chicken Wrapped in Lettuce Leaves

(Gai Yuk Sang Choy Bau)

This is my version of a traditional wrapped dish that can be found throughout China. Usually made with squab, it is cooked with vegetables and served hot wrapped in lettuce. What I have done is prepare the filling from diced roasted chicken meat, and rather than cook it further, I combine the diced chicken with all of its fresh accompaniments and serve the lettuce-wrapped rolls at a cool temperature. Until recently, fennel was unknown in most of China, except in Hong Kong, where it is used often in stir-fries as much for its crisp texture as for its distinctive taste. I have added it to this recipe for the same reasons. This is a fine warm weather dish.

1 cup roasted chicken meat cut into
   ¼-inch dice
¼ cup steamed black mushrooms
   (page 42) cut into ¼-inch dice
⅓ cup fennel from the center of the
   bulb cut into ¼-inch dice
¼ cup peeled fresh water chestnuts
   cut into ¼-inch dice
¼ cup red bell pepper cut into
   ¼-inch dice

2 teaspoons onion oil (page 39)
½ teaspoon salt
1½ teaspoons sugar
2 teaspoons Chinese white wine
   vinegar or distilled vinegar
1 teaspoon Shao-Hsing wine or
   sherry
6 large iceberg lettuce leaves, cut
   into rounds 5 inches in
   diameter

Put all the ingredients except the lettuce leaves in a large bowl and toss well to combine. Serve by spooning the mixture into the lettuce leaves and folding the ends to enclose the filling. Eat with your hands and serve with fingerbowls.

MAKES 4 TO 6 SERVINGS

Tea Eggs

(Cha Yip Don)

This fetching, simple dish is from Shanghai, where it is a custom for children to color eggs, quite like Western children do at Easter. The tea egg is a hard-boiled egg colored with and flavored by tea and a combination of spices. What makes it special is how it is made. The shell of the egg, after being hard-boiled, is lightly tapped to crack it and create a network of lines on its surface. After being immersed in its colorings and flavorings, the shell is removed and the shiny, peeled egg looks as if it is made of marble. A wonderful treat and one that is regularly offered as an appetizer.

3¼ cups cold water
1 cinnamon stick, broken into pieces
3 whole eight-star anise
10 cloves
¼ teaspoon anise seeds
2 teaspoons salt

½ cup black tea leaves
8 extra large eggs, hard-boiled, cooled, shells tapped gently with the back of spoon to create a network of cracks (care should be taken not to break through the shell)

Put the water, cinnamon stick, star anise, cloves, anise seeds, and salt in a pot, cover, and bring to a boil over high heat. Lower the heat and simmer for 15 minutes. Return the heat to high and bring to a boil. Add the tea leaves and stir well. Allow to cook for 2 minutes until the liquid becomes very dark. Add the cracked eggs to the liquid, turning them over several times. Lower the heat and simmer, covered, for 10 minutes. Turn off the heat and allow the eggs to sit in the liquid until sufficiently cool to handle. Peel each egg to reveal the marblization. Serve them whole, individually, or place in a bowl in the center of the table.

Makes 8 eggs

Note: The mixture of spices and tea is strong enough to color and flavor up to a dozen eggs.

Chicken in Soups

鷄湯類

*I*t would be difficult to find a culture on this earth that does not adore chicken soup, which is, depending upon one's point of view, nutritious, delicious, restorative, folk medicine, a mystical cure-all, and even spiritual. In my small world of Siu Lo Chen, chicken soup was liquid treasure, as well and a brew of traditional richness.

In China, soups of various sorts are said to correct or restore one's inner balance, to halt the graying of hair, and to clear congestion. Herbalists would even concoct mixes to brew with our chicken soup to improve our health. We had no vitamin pills or supplements; what we had was chicken soup, often cooked for many hours in a closed clay pot, so that none of its aroma, flavor, or inherent nutrition would dissipate.

Chickens provided meat and soup for our family. We even raised "black chickens," with black skin and flesh, so-called *juk see gai,* or "bamboo chickens." These we never ate; rather, they were only to be boiled for the longest time with ginseng root and drunk for our health.

Oddly, chicken soups were not given to babies or to the very young, for they were deemed too rich. Usually chicken soup was not fed to children until they were older. Chicken soup for the elderly was, however, a must. Chicken soup was usually eaten with the chicken with which it had been made, and often we would market twice a day to obtain fresh chickens.

At a banquet of many dishes soup is never eaten at the beginning of the meal. In our home, at smaller meals, we would eat soup at the outset of the meal, where it was served to satisfy initial hunger. At a banquet, it was believed, one's guests ought not to be filled initially with soup. One was served different dishes, with soup offered in mid-meal, to help digestion and to cleanse palates.

When I first came to Hong Kong from Siu Lo Chen, I lived with my number five aunt, Ng Gu Jeh, who operated a small sundries shop in Kowloon. She was known in the community as Ng Gah Jeh, or "Number Five Sister," or as Ng Gu, short for "Miss Five." She was famous for her Sunday soups, around which much

79

of the family gathered. Her soups were rich with chicken, chicken bones, and chicken feet, with mushrooms, lotus root, and all manner of vegetables afloat in it. It is a delicious memory.

Chicken soup, with a fine, intense stock as its base, or with pieces of chicken added to it, was and is the ultimate family food. It is my thought that it ought never be ladled into bowls and served individually. Rather, it should be brought to the table in large tureens, from which bowls are filled. In my home we even ate soup as a kind of sauce, poured over cooked rice. I recommend it highly.

Chicken soups, in addition, are marvelously accommodating hosts. They accept all sorts of ingredients with ease to the advantages of both.

Hot and Sour Soup

(Seun Lot Tong)

Is there a more well-known soup in China than hot and sour? Surely not. This soup, which began its existence in western China, in Hunan and Sichuan, has become universal in China, and everywhere else for that matter. Although it is usually made with pork, I have devised a hot and sour soup with chicken, which is just as delicious. This recipe has many ingredients, illustrative of how accommodating chicken soup can be. It is a simple dish, which asks only that you prepare all of your ingredients before cooking.

6 ounces chicken cutlets, cleaned thoroughly, dried and julienned

FOR THE MARINADE
½ teaspoon salt
1 teaspoon light soy sauce
1 teaspoon sesame oil
1½ teaspoons sugar
2 teaspoons cornstarch
Pinch white pepper
2 teaspoons Shao-Hsing wine or sherry

5 cups chicken stock (page 36)
1½ teaspoons minced garlic
1½ teaspoons minced ginger

2 tablespoons cloud ears, soaked in hot water for 20 minutes until soft, washed and drained
40 dried tiger lily buds, soaked in hot water for 20 minutes until soft, ends removed, and cut in half
½ cup shredded bamboo shoots
1 tablespoon hot red pepper flakes
4 tablespoons red wine vinegar
4 tablespoons cornstarch mixed with 4 tablespoons cold water
3 eggs, beaten with pinch of white pepper
2 cakes fresh bean curd, cut into ¼-inch-thick strips
1 tablespoon double dark soy sauce
2 tablespoons finely sliced scallions

Mix the marinade ingredients in a bowl. Add the chicken and mix well. Allow to rest for 20 minutes.

Pour the chicken stock into a large pot and add the garlic and ginger. Cover and bring to a boil over high heat. Add the cloud ears, tiger lily buds, bamboo shoots, pepper flakes, and vinegar and return to a boil. Cover, lower the heat, and simmer for 7 minutes. Return the heat to high and add the chicken with the marinade. Loosen the chicken and return to a boil. Add the cornstarch mixture, pouring slowly with one hand and stirring with a ladle in one direction with the other hand. When the soup thickens and returns to a boil, add the beaten egg in the same manner, pouring with one hand, stirring with the other. When the soup again returns to a boil, add the bean curd, stirring well. When the soup boils again, add the soy sauce and stir.

Turn off the heat. Transfer the soup to a heated tureen. Sprinkle with scallions and serve.

MAKES 4 TO 6 SERVINGS

Grated Winter Melon Soup with Minced Chicken

(Dong Gua Yung)

This is an unusual way of using winter melon, that very special melon of South China. Usually eaten in soups or stir-fried in chunks with other ingredients, in this classic dish from Guangdong the melon is grated into what is often called a "velvet" texture. Because of its capacity to take on the flavors of whatever it is cooked with, the grated melon becomes virtually a pureed chicken stock. This silken soup is perfect when blended with ground chicken.

½ pound chicken cutlets, cleaned thoroughly, dried, and ground

FOR THE MARINADE
½ teaspoon ginger juice, mixed with 1 tablespoon Chinese white rice wine or gin
3 teaspoons oyster sauce
3 teaspoons sesame oil
½ teaspoon salt
1 teaspoon sugar
4 teaspoons cornstarch
Pinch white pepper
2 egg whites, beaten

2½ pounds winter melon, peeled, seeded, and grated
4 cups chicken stock (page 36)
1 slice ginger, ½ inch long, lightly smashed
2 tablespoons Chinese white rice wine or gin
½ teaspoon salt
1½ teaspoons sugar
Pinch white pepper
⅓ cup finely sliced scallions, green parts only

Combine all the marinade ingredients in a bowl and mix well.

Put the chicken in the marinade and mix well. Allow to rest for 20 minutes.

Place the winter melon in a pot with the chicken stock, ginger, wine, salt, sugar, and white pepper and stir to mix well. Cover and bring to a boil over high heat. Lower the heat and simmer until the winter melon is very soft. Raise the heat to high and add the ground chicken and marinade. Stir, separating the chicken with a ladle. Allow to return to a boil. Boil for a minute. Taste for seasoning. Turn off the heat and transfer the soup to a heated tureen. Sprinkle with the scallions and serve.

MAKES 4 TO 6 SERVINGS

NOTE: There is no need to buy a whole melon, usually the size of a watermelon. It can be bought by weight, by the slice. This soup can be prepared 3 to 4 hours before serving. However, do not add scallions until ready to serve.

Cucumber and Chicken Soup

(Gai Yuk Ching Guah Tong)

This recipe is pure home cooking. Cucumbers are common and plentiful in China, where they often have three growing seasons. They find their way into stir-fries and stews; they are often braised, stuffed, and made into salads and soups. This soup is considered yin, a cooling soup, perfect for the warm months and for lowering body heat.

FOR THE MARINADE
- ³⁄₄ teaspoon salt
- 2 teaspoons sugar
- 1¹⁄₂ tablespoons oyster sauce
- 1 teaspoon sesame oil
- ¹⁄₈ teaspoon white pepper
- 1¹⁄₂ teaspoons cornstarch

- 4 cups chicken stock (page 36)
- 1¹⁄₂ cups cold water

- 2 large cucumbers (1³⁄₄ pounds) peeled, seeded, and cut into ¹⁄₂-inch cubes, to yield 3¹⁄₂ cups
- 1 slice ginger, ¹⁄₂ inch long, peeled, lightly smashed
- ³⁄₄ teaspoon salt
- 1¹⁄₂ tablespoons onion oil (page 39)
- 12 ounces chicken cutlets, cleaned thoroughly, dried, and cut into ¹⁄₂-inch dice

Mix the marinade ingredients in a bowl, add the chicken, toss to combine, and coat well. Allow to rest for 20 minutes.

In a large pot put the chicken stock and water, the prepared cucumbers, and the remaining ingredients except the chicken. Stir to mix well. Cover and bring to a boil over high heat. Lower the heat to medium and cook for 1¹⁄₂ to 2 minutes or until the cucumbers are tender. Return the heat to high. Add the chicken and marinade and stir, separating the chicken pieces. Allow the soup to return to a boil. Cook for 30 to 40 seconds until the chicken is cooked through. Turn off the heat. Transfer the soup to a heated tureen and serve.

MAKES 4 TO 6 SERVINGS

Corn Soup with Chicken

(Suk Mai Gai Tong)

This traditional soup, so familiar in Chinese restaurants, is usually a thin soup, made with canned creamed corn boiled in water. A creditable version can be made with canned corn, but I prefer fresh corn, and you will, too. This soup is almost a puree, quite like a chowder.

1 pound fresh corn kernels,
  preferably sliced from fresh ears
4½ cups chicken stock (page 36)

FOR THE MARINADE
2 egg whites, beaten
½ teaspoon salt
1 teaspoon sugar
2 teaspoons sesame oil

½ pound chicken cutlets, cleaned
  thoroughly, dried, and cut into
  ¼-inch dice
1 teaspoon grated ginger
⅛ teaspoon white pepper
2½ tablespoons cornstarch mixed
  with 2½ tablespoons water
⅓ cup finely sliced scallions

Put the corn kernels and a cup of the chicken stock in a blender and process to a coarse puree. Reserve.

Mix the marinade ingredients in a bowl and add the chicken. Toss to coat well. Allow the mixture to rest for 20 minutes. Put the remaining stock in a pot with the ginger and white pepper. Cover and bring to a boil over high heat. Add the pureed corn mixture and stir. Cover the pot, lower the heat, and simmer, leaving the lid partially open, for 5 minutes. Return the heat to high and add the chicken and marinade. Stir well, separating the chicken pieces. Allow to return to a boil. Lower the heat and simmer for 3 minutes, stirring frequently to prevent sticking. Raise the heat to high and add the cornstarch mixture slowly with one hand, stirring with the other to ensure smoothness. Cook until the soup thickens and bubbles. Turn off the heat. Taste for seasoning. Transfer to a heated tureen, sprinkle with scallions, and serve.

MAKES 4 TO 6 SERVINGS

Watercress Soup with Chicken Meatballs

(Sai Yeung Choi Gai Yeun Tong)

The Hakka, the Chinese nomads, are famous for using foods that have been minced or ground, formed into balls, and then cooked in various ways. Their fellow immigrants in southern China, the Chiu Chow, who make balls of beef, shrimp, fish, and cuttlefish, are known for their cooking methods as well. Chicken is seldom used in these dishes, so I have altered a classic Hakka dish to make these famous balls with chicken meat. Unfortunately in both cultures, these food balls are usually dense, hard, and rubbery, the result of overmixing. You can make tender balls at home simply by following these procedures.

1 recipe basic minced chicken filling
   (page 41)
2½ cups chicken stock
   (page 36)
2½ cups water

1 slice ginger, ½ inch long, lightly
   smashed
3 large bunches fresh watercress,
   each bunch cut in half, washed,
   and drained thoroughly

Make the chicken meatballs: Form the filling into a loose ball and throw it against the side of a bowl. Repeat eight to ten times to make the mix cohesive. Wet your hands with water and divide the filling into 20 equal parts. Put the mixture in a dish moistened so the meat will not stick. Form 20 meatballs. Wet your hands occasionally as you form the meatballs to prevent sticking.

Put the stock, water, and ginger in a pot, cover, and bring to a boil over high heat. Add the meatballs and allow the soup to return to a boil. When the meatballs float to the top they are cooked. Add the watercress and allow the soup to return to a boil. Turn off the heat. Transfer soup to a preheated tureen and serve immediately.

Makes 4 to 6 servings

Note: Watercress must always be cooked in boiling liquid, otherwise it becomes bitter.

Chiu Chow Rice Noodle Soup

(Chiu Chow Guor Tiu)

Again, a classic reworked. This famous Chiu Chow preparation is based on a good chicken stock and fettuccini-like rice noodles. This soup, with its chicken meatballs, is indeed hearty and is the traditional luncheon of many Chiu Chow people. Occasionally made in the home, it is usually eaten in restaurants accompanied by glasses of strong hot tea.

8 cups cold water	3½ cups chicken stock (page 36)
8 ounces rice noodles	1½ tablespoons minced Tianjin
1 recipe basic minced chicken filling	preserved vegetable
(page 41)	2 cups finely sliced iceberg lettuce

Pour the water in a pot and bring to a boil over high heat. Add the rice noodles and stir with a wooden spoon, making certain the noodles are completely immersed. Cook, stirring, for 2½ to 3 minutes or until the noodles are cooked al dente. Do not overcook. Turn off the heat, run cold water into the pot, and drain. Repeat. Reserve the noodles.

Make 16 chicken meatballs, using the same process as in the preceding recipe. Reserve.

Put the chicken stock in a pot with the Tianjin preserved vegetable, cover, and bring to a boil over high heat. Add the meatballs and allow the stock to return to a boil. Cook until the meatballs float to the top. Add the lettuce and reserved noodles and stir well. Allow the soup to return to a boil. Turn off the heat, transfer to a preheated tureen and serve immediately.

Makes 4 servings

Note: This Chiu Chow soup tastes best and is most authentic with the minced Tianjin preserved vegetable, which has an intense garlic and salt flavor. There is no substitute, so if it is unavailable, add 2 teaspoons minced garlic and ¼ teaspoon salt to the soup.

Egg Drop Soup

(DON FAR TONG)

蛋花湯

Which came first, the chicken or the egg? In certain parts of China the answer would be the soup. But which soup, chicken soup or egg drop soup? It is a dilemma. This simple soup, which translates as "egg flowers soup," must be made from the freshest ingredients: good stock, fresh eggs, scallions just out of the ground. Transplanted to the West, and a staple in virtually every Chinese restaurant extant, it has become dull, often thickened with eggs simply tossed in, causing lumps. What follows is the true don far tong, *in which the beaten eggs, poured slowly, become, as the name suggests, like flowers.*

6 cups chicken stock
  (page 36)
½ teaspoon salt

6 extra large eggs, at room
  temperature, beaten
½ cup finely sliced scallions

Put the stock and salt in a large pot, cover, and bring to a boil over high heat. Gradually pour in the beaten eggs in a steady stream with one hand, and with the other hand whisk constantly with a large cooking fork until soft, silken threads of egg form, about a minute. Turn off the heat. Transfer the soup to a preheated tureen. Gently mound the scallions in the center of the soup, and serve.

MAKES 4 TO 6 SERVINGS

Spinach Soup with Chicken and Bean Threads

(BOR CHOI GAI SEE TONG)

This is a traditional recipe in Chinese homes. In our house, in childhood and today, this was and is a winter soup, one that warms and stays with you long after you've eaten it. We often added different ingredients for variety, but the base was always chicken stock, spinach, and bean threads.

FOR THE MARINADE
- 2 teaspoons sesame oil
- 1 tablespoon Shao-Hsing wine or sherry
- 1/4 teaspoon salt
- 1 teaspoon sugar
- Pinch white pepper

- 8 ounces chicken cutlet, cleaned thoroughly, dried, and cut into 2 1/2-inch-long by 1/4-inch-long julienne

- 1 ounce bean thread noodles
- 4 cups hot water
- 5 cups chicken stock (page 36)
- 1 tablespoon Shao-Hsing wine or sherry
- 1 tablespoon minced ginger
- 1/2 teaspoon salt
- 1 pound spinach, washed thoroughly and drained well, leaves broken in half

Mix the marinade ingredients in a bowl and add the chicken. Toss to coat well. Allow the mixture to rest for 20 minutes. Soak the bean threads in hot water for 20 minutes and drain. Cut the threads into manageable lengths and reserve.

Put the stock in a large pot and add the wine, ginger, and salt. Cover and bring to a boil over high heat. Add the spinach and stir until it is completely immersed in stock. Return to a boil. Add the chicken and marinade and stir, separating the chicken pieces. Allow to return to a boil. Add the bean threads, stirring well to separate the strands and return to a boil. Turn off the heat and taste for seasoning. Transfer the soup to a preheated tureen and serve.

MAKES 4 TO 6 SERVINGS

Tomato, Potato, and Chicken Soup

(Fan Keh Soo Jai Gai Tong)

When I tell people I ate this soup quite often as a child in China, they are generally surprised, because the tomato and the white potato, assuredly Western vegetables, are not thought of as being ingredients in Chinese cooking. They are, however. The sweet potato came to China in the 1500s during the Ming dynasty; the white potato followed two centuries later during the Qing dynasty; and the tomato arrived about one hundred years ago. As with most vegetables they were embraced in the fertile south and became important crops. This soup was a favorite of my father. I stress that for this fragrant, slightly thick soup, the tomatoes must be very ripe.

12 ounces chicken cutlets, cleaned thoroughly, dried, and cut into ½-inch dice

FOR THE MARINADE
1 teaspoon light soy sauce
1½ tablespoons oyster sauce
½ teaspoon salt
2 teaspoons sugar
½ tablespoon Shao-Hsing wine or sherry
1 tablespoon cornstarch

2 tablespoons peanut oil
2 teaspoons salt
1½ teaspoons minced ginger
1½ teaspoons minced garlic
4 cups fresh ripe tomatoes, peeled and cut into ½-inch cubes
3 cups fresh potatoes, peeled and cut into ½-inch cubes
2½ cups chicken stock (page 36)
3 cups cold water

Put the chicken and marinade ingredients in a bowl, mix well, and marinate for an hour.

Heat a wok over high heat for 40 seconds. Add the peanut oil and coat the wok with it, using a spatula. Add the salt, ginger, and garlic and stir for 30 seconds. Add the tomatoes and stir-fry for a minute. Add the potatoes and stir for 2 minutes until all the ingredients are blended. Transfer the contents to a large pot.

Add the stock and water to the pot and stir to mix. Cover and bring to a boil over high heat. Lower the heat and simmer for 30 minutes until the potatoes are softened, stirring occasionally. Return the heat to high and add the chicken and marinade, making certain to separate the chicken pieces when stirring. Allow the soup to return to a boil and cook for 2 minutes until the chicken is cooked through. Turn off the heat. Transfer the soup to a preheated tureen and serve.

Makes 4 to 6 servings

Minced Chicken Soup

(Gai Yuk Gung)

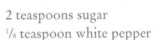

The texture of this soup is of utmost importance, a peculiarly Chinese tradition. In Chinese cooking there are soups commonly called tong, *and there are others referred to as* gung. *A gung is thickened, just short of being a puree. Soups can be any combination of ingredients with stock. Gung usually consist of stock thickened with tapioca starch to which ingredients are added. This is a classic gung.*

8 ounces chicken cutlet, cleaned
    thoroughly, dried, and ground

FOR THE CHICKEN MIXTURE
1 tablespoon tapioca starch
1/2 cup chicken stock
    (page 36)
1 tablespoon Chinese white rice
    wine or gin
1 teaspoon light soy sauce
1/2 teaspoon salt

2 teaspoons sugar
1/8 teaspoon white pepper

3 cups chicken stock
1 1/2 cups cold water
1 tablespoon minced ginger
4 tablespoons tapioca starch mixed
    with 5 tablespoons cold water
3 tablespoons finely sliced fresh
    coriander
3 tablespoons finely sliced scallions

Place the ground chicken in a bowl. Add the chicken mixture and stir until a puree-like texture is reached.

Put the chicken stock, cold water, and ginger in a pot, and cover. Bring to a boil over high heat. Stir the chicken mixture and pour it into the pot slowly with one hand, stirring with the other. Allow the mixture to return to a boil. Stir the tapioca starch–water mixture and pour it into the pot slowly, again with one hand, while stirring with the other to ensure smoothness. Allow the soup to return to a boil. Turn off the heat. Transfer to a preheated tureen. Sprinkle with coriander and scallions and serve.

MAKES 4 SERVINGS

Rice with Chicken, Chicken with Rice

鷄飯粥類

*R*ice is China's national staple. China has grown rice for five thousand years and today accounts for a third of the world's rice crop, virtually all of which is consumed domestically. Not only is rice an essential of Chinese life, it is a metaphor as well. If one is invited to dine in a Chinese home, one is asked to *sik fan,* or "eat rice." If a family is provided for and well fed, it is said to have a full rice bowl; if poor, its rice bowl is empty.

Symbolically, in most Chinese homes, including mine in our Sun Tak village, there was always a bowl of uncooked rice displayed—in our case one of elaborately carved red lacquer, which during New Year's the word's *seung moon,* or "always full" were taped. Small bowls of cooked rice were always part of our family's offerings of food to our ancestors during temple visits.

Rice is eaten in many ways. It is cooked with water or with stock, it is steamed, boiled, fried, and made into congees; it is the filling for dumplings and pastries. Fresh and dried noodles are made from rice flour and it is wrapped in bundles with lotus or bamboo leaves. Rice is a stuffing for chickens, and when sweetened with preserved and candied fruits, it is the basis for special occasion cakes.

Varieties of rice abound in China. There is, of course, white rice, short, medium, and long grain, with the last, including extra long-grain rice, considered the best and most elegant. Generally, that is the rice I recommend in this book, except when different grains are specified. Extra long-grain rice is also grown in the United States, notably in Texas, and also in Thailand, where it is scented with jasmine. The latter is a fine rice and can be used in any recipe that calls for extra long-grain rice. When extra long-grain rice is cooked properly, its grains are separated individually and fluffy. Very little brown rice—rice partially milled with its brown chaff left intact—is eaten in China, where white rice is valued esthetically.

Medium-grain rice is eaten widely in China as well but is favored by those

who like their rice with a softer consistency. Short-grain rice cooks even softer—its grains tend to stick together in clumps when cooked—but it is perfect for congees when combined with glutinous rice, another variety of short-grain rice. Glutinous rice, often called "sweet rice" or "sticky rice" because of its consistency after cooking, is also used for molds and stuffings and is the rice of choice in the Chinese sweet cake.

The Chinese regard rice in the way a Westerner regards bread. In our home, when I was growing up, we ate rice three times a day and often with chicken prepared in various ways and with chicken soup. We had our own chickens for eggs, some of which we raised from chicks, others which we bought as chicks from vendors. Grown, they provided us with eggs, for ten months to a year before they became bases for stocks, soups, and for stir-fries and other cooked dishes. Their eggs were often preserved in a salt solution, or cured, to be eaten as condiments, always with rice.

In this chapter, chicken and rice are partners. Chickens flavor rice, are additions to rice dishes, are steamed with rice, and are cooked together with rice, as the Chinese have been doing for centuries.

Congee

(Jook)

Congee is understood these days to be a rice gruel or porridge, eaten most often at breakfast and generally with other ingredients added to it for taste and texture. Congee is a dish enjoyed in every corner of China. Its name in this context means "soft rice," and made with water it is considered most nourishing for the very young and the very old. Babies are raised on it and the elderly like it for the ease with which it can be digested.

It can be eaten with various vegetables, fish, or meats; it can be sweetened with rock sugar, one of the ways it is eaten in Guangzhou; or served as a savory mix with seasoned cabbage, as in Shanghai.

Historically in northwest China, congees were made with different bases—wheat, barley, sorghum, millet, tapioca, and later corn—sometimes in combination with rice, sometimes not. But in its most familiar form, congee is made with rice. In the thousand years of its existence, congees have been flavored with pears, chrysanthemums, ginger, ginseng, lotus leaves, and mint. Today's congee is a mix of short-grain and glutinous rices, and its most common accompaniments are chicken, fish, vegetables, preserved eggs, and herbs.

As with so many of China's traditional foods, there is a delightful folk tale concerning congee. Once a miserly man, faced with the need but not the will to provide rice for ten guests, told his cook to stretch the rice by ladling water into the rice as it cooked. He would do this, he told his cook, by calling the cook's name, Ah Fook. His name, spoken aloud, was the signal to add a ladle of water to the rice. However, even before the arrival of his guests, the miser, called to his cook on other matters and with each call of his name came a ladleful of water into the rice, for the cook was an obedient man. The result was a thin porridge rather than cooked rice, and in a rhyme—"Ah Fook, Ah Fook, Ah Fook, Ah Fook. Fook mut yeh, bin jor wok jook" (which translates as the miser calling the cook)—the cook becomes angry as his rice turns to porridge. When I was a child we used to chant this rhyme and laugh. To us it meant that we should not be selfish.

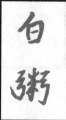

Basic White Congee

(Bak Jook)

½ cup short-grain white
¼ cup glutinous rice
4½ cups cold water

4 cups chicken stock (page 36)
Salt

Put both rices in a large pot. Cover with cold water. Wash the rice three times by rubbing the grains between your palms and drain.

Return the washed rice to the pot and add the water and chicken stock. Bring to a boil over high heat. Cover the pot, leaving the lid slightly open. Lower the heat to medium-low and cook, stirring occasionally to prevent sticking. Cook until the rice thickens to the consistency of porridge, about an hour. Add salt to taste. Turn off the heat. Transfer the congee to a preheated tureen and serve.

MAKES 4 SERVINGS

Chicken Congee

(Gai Jook)

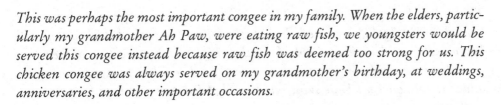

This was perhaps the most important congee in my family. When the elders, particularly my grandmother Ah Paw, were eating raw fish, we youngsters would be served this congee instead because raw fish was deemed too strong for us. This chicken congee was always served on my grandmother's birthday, at weddings, anniversaries, and other important occasions.

FOR THE MARINADE
- 3 teaspoons light soy sauce
- 3 teaspoons Shao-Hsing wine or sherry
- 3 teaspoons cornstarch
- 2 teaspoons sugar
- 1/2 teaspoon salt
- 2 tablespoons finely shredded ginger
- 2 tablespoons scallion oil (page 38)
- 1/8 teaspoon white pepper

- 1 pound chicken cutlet, cleaned thoroughly, dried, and thinly sliced into 2-inch-long pieces
- 1 recipe basic white congee (page 98)
- 3 tablespoons finely sliced scallions, green parts only, for garnish

Mix the marinade in a bowl, add the chicken pieces, and allow to rest for 20 minutes.

Prepare the basic congee. When it is thickened, raise the heat to high. Add the chicken and marinade and stir. Allow the congee to return to a boil. Lower the heat and simmer for 2 minutes until the chicken is cooked through. Turn off the heat. Transfer the congee to a preheated tureen. Sprinkle scallions on top and serve.

MAKES 4 SERVINGS

Gold and Silver Chicken Congee

(Gum Ngan Gai Jook)

This unusual congee recipe is one I learned in Ningbo, a sprawling city near Shanghai. The "gold" is roasted chicken, the "silver" uncooked chicken that will become white with cooking. Cooked together they are a treasure. One of the many garnishes eaten with congees are savory, deep-fried "crullers," cut into pieces and added to the congee. I have substituted crisply fried won ton strips for texture as well as taste.

4 cups peanut oil
12 won ton wrappers, cut into
    ½-inch-wide strips
1 recipe basic white congee
    (page 98)
2 tablespoons finely shredded
    ginger
8 ounces chicken cutlet, cleaned
    thoroughly, dried, and cut into
    2½-inch-long fine julienne

1½ cups roasted chicken (page 60)
    cut into 2½-inch-long fine
    julienne
1 tablespoon sesame oil
1 tablespoon light soy sauce
⅛ teaspoon white pepper
Salt, optional
3 tablespoons finely sliced scallions
2 tablespoons finely sliced fresh
    coriander

Heat a wok over high heat for a minute and add the peanut oil. When a wisp of white smoke appears, add the won ton strips. Deep-fry until golden brown, 45 seconds to a minute. Turn off the heat. Remove with a strainer and drain on paper towels. Reserve.

Prepare the basic congee. When it is thickened, raise the heat to high, add the ginger, and stir. Add the uncooked chicken and stir, bringing the congee back to a boil. Add the roasted chicken and stir. Add the sesame oil, soy sauce, and white pepper and stir. Allow the congee to return to a boil. Taste for seasoning and add salt if desired. Turn off the heat, add the scallions, and stir. Transfer to a preheated tureen, sprinkle with coriander, and serve with the won ton strips in small individual dishes.

Makes 4 servings

Note: The won ton strips may be made up to two days in advance. Fry and drain them well, allow to cool, and place in a tightly sealed plastic container.

Lotus Leaf Rice with Chicken

(Siu Gai Hor Yip Fan)

This preparation exists in many versions in China. The subtle flavor imparted by the lotus leaf when steamed with rice is delicious indeed, and the combination of the two is favored by virtually all chefs, who create new dishes from this traditional base. Different recipes call for glutinous rice surrounding such fillings as Chinese sausages, pork, shrimp, mushrooms, and of course, chicken. The version I have designed uses chicken and my steamed black mushrooms with glutinous rice.

1½ cups glutinous rice
1½ cups cold water
¼ teaspoon salt
1½ teaspoons minced ginger
1½ teaspoons minced garlic
1½ cups roasted chicken (page 60) cut into ¼-inch dice
½ cup steamed black mushrooms (page 42) cut into ¼-inch dice
1 tablespoon Shao-Hsing wine or sherry

4 fresh water chestnuts, peeled, washed, dried, and cut into ¼-inch dice
½ cup finely sliced scallions
1½ tablespoons oyster sauce
2½ tablespoons white peppercorn oil (page 39)
1 teaspoon sugar
2 teaspoons light soy sauce
Pinch white pepper

2 large lotus leaves, soaked in hot water for 30 minutes until softened, then rinsed

Put the rice in a pot and add enough water to cover. Wash and drain the rice three times by rubbing it between your palms. Place the rice in a round cake pan 8 inches in diameter and add the cold water. Place the pan in a steamer and steam for 30 to 40 minutes until the rice is cooked. Turn off the heat.

Put the steamed rice and remaining ingredients except the lotus leaves in a bowl and mix well. Wipe the lotus leaves dry. Place flat on a work surface, one on top of the other, so that no holes show through. Mound the rice mixture in the center of the leaves and fold inward on one side, then the other. Repeat with the other two sides to create a bundle.

Place the bundles in a steamer, folded side down, and steam for 30 to 40 minutes, or until heated through. Turn off the heat. Transfer the steamer to a large platter and serve by cutting a round hole in the leaves with kitchen shears and spooning the rice onto plates.

MAKES 4 SERVINGS

NOTE: This dish may be prepared through the second paragraph of the instructions up to 2 days in advance and refrigerated. Before steaming allow the bundles to come to room temperature, then proceed with the recipe.

Steamed Chicken with Roasted Rice

(Fun Jing Gai)

This method of preparing chicken with rice is a Sichuan classic. At its core is roasted rice, which gives the dish its special flavor. Dry-roasting is usually reserved for nuts and seeds rather than for grains of rice, but when roasted the rice gives off a delicate, elegant fragrance.

1 cup short-grain rice
12 ounces chicken cutlet, cleaned thoroughly, dried, and cut into 2-inch-long by ¼-inch-wide pieces
1½ tablespoons hoisin sauce
2½ teaspoons sugar
2 teaspoons light soy sauce
2 teaspoons sesame oil
1½ teaspoons minced ginger

4 scallions, trimmed and finely sliced, plus 3 tablespoons green parts as garnish
3 tablespoons Shao-Hsing wine or sherry
⅛ teaspoon salt
1 tablespoon Tabasco sauce
Pinch white pepper
1½ tablespoons peanut oil
½ cup chicken stock (page 36)

Prepare the roasted rice. Put the rice in a bowl, cover with water, and wash and drain the rice three times by rubbing it between your palms. Soak for an hour, drain, and allow to dry thoroughly. Heat a wok over high heat for 20 seconds and add the rice, spreading it in a thin layer. Lower the heat to medium and dry-roast (see page 16) until golden brown. Turn off the heat. When the rice cools, place it in a blender and grind coarsely. Reserve.

While the rice soaks and dries, prepare the chicken. Place it and all the other ingredients except the scallions in a bowl. Toss to coat well and allow to rest for an hour. Add the reserved roasted rice to the bowl and mix well.

Place the mixture in a steamproof dish. Place the dish in a steamer and steam for 20 minutes until the chicken cooks through. Halfway through the process, turn the chicken over. Turn off the heat. Place the chicken on a platter. Sprinkle with the sliced scallions and serve.

MAKES 4 SERVINGS

NOTE: Roasted rice may be prepared in advance. It will keep, stored in a closed jar in a cool, dry place, for at least 2 months.

RICE WITH CHICKEN, CHICKEN WITH RICE

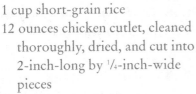

Fried Rice

(Chau Fan)

This ubiquitous Chinese preparation has an interesting history. Originally it was a way to reuse leftover cooked rice. This rice was usually stir-fried in a wok with beaten eggs and always with scallions and coriander. Over the years, it evolved into a preparation of many and varied ingredients, not only with leftover rice, but with rice cooked specifically for the purpose of making fried rice. It is not necessary but is preferable for the rice to cool to room temperature. The recipes that follow illustrate how many different ingredients work well with rice fried in a wok.

Chicken Fried Rice with Sun-Dried Tomatoes

(Tai Gawn Keh Gai Chau Fan)

This fried rice immediately pleases the eye with the vivid red sun-dried tomatoes.

1 recipe perfect cooked rice
(page 37)
4 extra large eggs, beaten with pinch
of white pepper and pinch of salt
4 tablespoons peanut oil

FOR THE SAUCE
2 tablespoons oyster sauce
1 tablespoon light soy sauce
1½ teaspoons Shao-Hsing wine or
sherry
1½ teaspoons sugar
¾ teaspoon salt

Pinch white pepper
1 teaspoon sesame oil

1½ teaspoons minced ginger
1 cup broccoli stems cut into
¼-inch dice
1½ cups roasted chicken (page 60)
cut into ¼-inch dice
¼ cup sun-dried tomatoes washed
in warm water and cut into
½ by ¼-inch pieces
½ cup finely sliced scallions
3 tablespoons minced fresh coriander

Prepare the basic rice recipe and allow the rice to cool to room temperature. As it cools, scramble the eggs in a tablespoon of the peanut oil over medium heat until cooked. Cut into small pieces and reserve. Combine the sauce ingredients in a bowl and reserve.

Heat a wok over high heat for 30 seconds. Add 2 tablespoons of the peanut oil and coat the wok with it, using a spatula. When a wisp of white smoke appears, add the ginger and stir briefly. Add the broccoli stems, stir, and cook for 20 seconds. Add the chicken and stir-fry for 30 seconds. Add the cooked rice and mix it well with the ginger and broccoli, turning and stirring, for 5 minutes until the rice mixture is very hot.

Stir the sauce and pour it over the rice and mix thoroughly. If the rice sticks, add the remaining tablespoon of peanut oil. Add the eggs and stir. And the sun-dried tomatoes and combine thoroughly. Add the scallions and coriander and mix well. Turn off the heat. Transfer the mixture to a preheated serving dish, and serve.

MAKES 4 SERVINGS

RICE WITH CHICKEN, CHICKEN WITH RICE

Fried Rice with Chicken and Asparagus

(HEUNG MAI LO SUN GAI CHAU FAN)

Asparagus is a recent addition to Chinese cooking and capers are rarely found in the Chinese kitchen. These two vegetables, "borrowed" from the West, illustrate the versatility of fried rice. Fried rice combinations are limited only by one's imagination.

1 recipe perfect cooked rice
   (page 37)
4 extra large eggs, beaten with pinch
   of white pepper and pinch of salt
4 tablespoons scallion oil (page 38)

FOR THE SAUCE

2 tablespoons oyster sauce
1 tablespoon light soy sauce
2 teaspoons Shao-Hsing wine or
   sherry
1½ teaspoons sugar
1 teaspoon sesame oil
Pinch white pepper

1½ teaspoons minced ginger
8 medium asparagus stalks, hard
   ends removed, cut across into
   ¼-inch slices
¼ cup capers
5 fresh water chestnuts, peeled and
   cut into ¼-inch dice (⅔ cup)
1½ cups poached chicken (page 61)
   cut into ¼-inch dice
2 tablespoons chicken stock
   (page 36)
3 scallions, trimmed and finely
   sliced
3 tablespoons minced fresh
   coriander

Prepare the basic cooked rice. Allow to cool to room temperature and reserve. Scramble the eggs with a tablespoon of the scallion oil over medium heat until cooked. Cut up the eggs coarsely and reserve. Combine the sauce ingredients in a bowl and reserve.

Heat a wok over high heat for 30 seconds. Add 2 tablespoons of the scallion oil and coat the wok with it, using a spatula. When a wisp of white smoke appears add the ginger and stir for 30 seconds until its fragrance is released. Add the asparagus and capers and stir and cook for a minute. Add the water chestnuts and stir, and then add the chicken and stir for 30 seconds. Add chicken stock and stir for 1 minute. Add the rice and mix thoroughly, making certain it is coated and very hot.

Add the eggs and stir them in. Stir the reserved sauce, and pour it into the rice, mixing well. Stir-fry for 2 more minutes. If the rice sticks add the remaining table-spoon of oil. Add the scallions and coriander and mix well. Turn off the heat. Transfer the rice to a preheated dish and serve.

NOTE: For this dish in particular, make the basic rice recipe with extra long-grain jasmine-scented rice from Thailand.

Hainan Chicken Rice

(Hoi Lam Gai Fan)

This is a dish with a long tradition from the Chinese who migrated from Hainan, an island off southernmost China, to Southeast Asia. Historically, these most daring voyagers sailed to, traded with, and settled mostly in areas that are now part of Malaysia and Singapore. This thoroughly Chinese preparation has become almost synonymous with Singapore, where it is still honored with the name Hainan. Its separate elements—cooked rice, cooked chicken, and a rich soup—are served together as a single course and eaten in any combination one wishes.

1 whole chicken (4 to 4½ pounds), cleaned thoroughly and dried, giblets reserved

3 tablespoons Chinese white rice wine or gin

2 teaspoons salt

5 onions (1¼ pounds), quartered

1 slice ginger, 1½ inches long, peeled, coarsely chopped

2 whole garlic cloves, peeled

18 sprigs fresh coriander, washed thoroughly

10 cups cold water

2 cups extra long-grain rice

Ginger garlic dip (recipe follows)

After cleaning, rinsing, and drying the chicken, rub it with the rice wine and sprinkle with salt, both outside and inside the cavity. Put the onions, ginger, garlic, 12 sprigs of the coriander, the giblets, and cold water in a casserole or Dutch oven. Cover and bring to a boil over high heat. Reduce the heat and simmer for 45 minutes, leaving the lid slightly open.

Add the chicken to the pot, breast side up. Increase the heat and return to a boil. Cover, reduce the heat to low, and simmer for 30 minutes, leaving the lid slightly open. Turn the chicken over and simmer for 15 minutes more. Turn the chicken breast side up again and simmer for another 15 minutes. Remove the pot from the heat, turn off the heat, and allow the chicken to rest in liquid, covered, for another 15 minutes. Transfer the chicken to a platter to cool sufficiently to handle. Strain the cooking liquid (now a soup), skim off the fat, and reserve.

While the chicken cooks, prepare the rice: Put the rice in a medium pot, add water to cover, and wash and drain the rice three times by rubbing the grains with your palms. Drain. Return the rice to the pot, add 2 cups of the reserved soup, and bring to a boil over high heat. Stir and cook until bubbles begin to appear on the surface, about 3 minutes. Reduce the heat to low, cover, and cook for 6 minutes. Stir, cover again, and cook until tender, 3 to 5 minutes. Turn off the heat. Transfer the rice to a preheated bowl.

Heat the remaining soup, cut up the chicken into bite-size pieces, place on a serving platter, and serve in the traditional manner by pouring the soup into six individual bowls and filling six other bowls with cooked rice. Serve the chicken, rice, and soup together, garnished with the remaining coriander and accompanied by the traditional intense ginger and garlic dip.

MAKES 6 SERVINGS

Ginger Garlic Dip

6 tablespoons peanut oil
4 tablespoons grated ginger
2 tablespoons minced garlic
1 1/2 teaspoons salt

Mix all the ingredients in a bowl and transfer to small individual condiment dishes.

MAKES 6 SERVINGS

Stir-Fried Glutinous Rice with Chicken

(Gai Lop Chau Nor Mai Fan)

This is a classic dish from Chinese teahouses, usually heralded by waitresses with their carts singing, "San chau nor mai fan." This phrase literally means combining all of the uncooked ingredients and then stir-frying them. The familiar smooth domed mounds of rice are the result. Glutinous rice is cooked with different ingredients, packed into a rice bowl and then turned over. My adaptation is to replace the customary Chinese bacon and sausage with chicken.

2 cups glutinous rice
2 cups cold water
8 cups boiling water
3 tablespoons onion oil (page 39)
3/4 teaspoon salt
1 cup roasted chicken (page 60) cut
 into 1/4-inch dice

FOR THE SAUCE

1 1/2 teaspoons light soy sauce
1 teaspoons dark soy sauce
3 1/2 tablespoons oyster sauce

1/2 cup finely sliced scallions
2 tablespoons finely sliced fresh
 coriander

Put the rice in a bowl and wash and drain the rice three times by rubbing the grains between your palms. Rinse and drain. Put the rice in an 8-inch cake pan and add the cold water. Place the cake pan in a steamer and cover. Pour the boiling water into a wok, place the steamer in the wok, and turn the heat to high. Steam the rice for 35 to 40 minutes until the rice becomes translucent. Transfer the rice to a bowl and allow it to cool. While it cools, mix the sauce ingredients in a bowl.

Heat a wok over high heat for 30 seconds. Add the oil and coat the wok with it, using a spatula. When a wisp of white smoke appears, add the salt and stir briefly. Add the rice, stir, and cook until the rice is very hot. Add the chicken and stir for a minute. Add the sauce, lower the heat to medium, and stir and mix, making certain the rice and chicken are evenly coated. Add the scallions and coriander, and stir. Turn off the heat.

Serve in the traditional manner by packing the rice into individual rice bowls and then upending them on heated plates to create perfect rounded mounds. Serve immediately.

MAKES 4 SERVINGS

Chicken Pearl Balls

(Gai Yuk Jun Jiu Kau)

This luminous dish is quite beautiful. After the pearl balls are steamed, the grains of glutinous rice adhering to them resemble tiny seed pearls. This dish is famous in Shanghai, where it is customarily made with pork as a dim sum and is often served with other dumplings. I have had it served as a first course in a banquet. My adaptation is to make it identically with tradition but to replace the pork with chicken. I have served these unusual "pearls" at dinners and buffets, with great success. They can be frozen and resteamed.

Double recipe basic minced chicken
    filling (page 41)
2 tablespoons chicken stock
    (page 36)

1½ cups glutinous rice
2 or 3 green lettuce leaves,
    sufficiently large to line a
    bamboo steamer

Put the chicken filling in a bowl, add the stock, and mix well. Refrigerate for at least 4 hours or overnight.

Put the rice in a bowl with water to cover. Wash and drain the rice three times by rubbing it between your palms. Drain, add water to cover, and allow the rice to soak for an hour. Drain the rice through a strainer for an additional hour. (The rice should be moist but not watery.) Spread the moist rice in a thin layer on a cookie sheet lined with waxed paper. On a second cookie sheet place a sheet of waxed paper brushed with peanut oil. Rub peanut oil on your hands and begin making the pearl balls.

Pick up a handful of the chicken mixture, move it around in your hand gently, and then squeeze. The amount that oozes through the top of your hand will make a ball about an inch in diameter. Repeat until all the mixture is used. (About 20 balls will be formed.) As you work, keep your hands oiled, to prevent sticking. Roll each ball of chicken through the rice and then place it on the oiled waxed paper. Repeat until all 20 chicken balls have been rolled.

Line a steamer with lettuce leaves. Place the pearl balls on the leaves and steam for about 20 minutes or until the rice grains become translucent and the chicken cooks through. Serve immediately by placing the steamer in a serving platter.

MAKES 20 PEARL BALLS

Rice with Chicken, Chicken with Rice

Chicken with Noodles, Dumplings, and Buns

*I*n China, foods fashioned from dough are traditionally called *mein fan* (literally "powdered wheat"), which includes all foods made from flour—noodles, breads, buns, pastries, cakes, and dumplings. Thus, noodles are *mein;* breads are *mein bau;* sweet breads are *tim mein bau;* and sweet cakes are *mein bang*. Dough made from this powdered wheat is *mein fan tun*, literally, "wheat flour formed into a pile."

In early China, these *mein fan* were usually described as "noodle foods" and were steamed, fried, and baked. This tradition of breads and other foods made from dough surprises many who think of China as a rice-based culture. Rice is dominant to be sure, but wheat was and is very important, particularly in the north, in and around Beijing.

The practice of creating dough from milled flours—not only from wheat, but from millet and barley as well—was born in the north, in the Beijing area, and throughout Shandong, where grains, not rice, were the staples of the diet. But as with all the foods of history, when people relocated and rice and the rice culture moved northward, the culture of wheat and its flour came south. These days there are no boundaries. Rice and wheat are embraced equally throughout China.

Chinese breadstuffs go back two thousand years to what are believed to be clay-baked flatbreads and steamed and fried breads of great variety. Early dough foods included unfilled breads eaten as accompaniments to other dishes, notably cooked vegetables, pork, and chicken, particularly in Beijing and Sichuan. Later they were sweet and savory, filled with honey, animal fats, sugar, and sweetened pastes. From the bread came the noodle, the shape and length of which came to symbolize long life. Like other foods of the Chinese kitchen, breads and noodles were and are offered at ancestral altars and temples.

The noodle moved south, west, and east, and became a universal ingredient. Breads are eaten with enjoyment, as are buns and dumplings, staples of the dim sum kitchen. Loaves are, to be sure, most important to the north. Southerners treasure those small teahouse foods, filled dumplings, stuffed and filled buns, and pastries, most of them steamed.

Traditionally, in the north or south, an accompaniment to noodles was and is chicken. Buns, steamed or baked, as well as baked pastries are filled with chicken. In this chapter I illustrate all aspects of China's *mein fan*—noodles of wheat and rice, boiled, fried, and in soups; small breads and buns, filled and unfilled, steamed and baked, as well as a selection of dumplings, the roots of which lie in the teahouse and the dim sum parlor.

When I was growing up, noodles were a great treat. We never made them at home, however. We always went to the noodle shop in our village for plates of noodles, usually mixed with shredded chicken, or bowls of soup with noodles, always served with mounds of cut-up roasted chicken on top. We would search for the longest noodle strands and suck them up very slowly, arguing who had the longest noodle, and therefore would live the longest life.

Our teahouse was a treat as well. My older brother, Ching Mo, who was very tall, would put me on his shoulders and we would go off to the teahouse for steamed dumplings and buns stuffed with a variety of fillings, including chicken. Steamed chicken buns were favorites of mine, and my brother always saw to it that I had several. Even better was the end of the early service in the teahouse when just before closing the proprietor would send out dumplings and buns that had not been sold and offer them for only pennies. We would eat them with the pieces of leftover chicken that had not been sold at a fraction of their usual price.

I relive these childhood memories from time to time in my head and in my mouth, and they always return when I am cooking noodles and making dumplings in my kitchen.

With some of the recipes in this section I specify a particular brand of flour. As you know, flours are quixotic. Some, ostensibly of the same mix, behave differently in different climates and temperatures and at different times of the year. It is not unusual for cooks and bakers who work constantly with flours to carry their favorite flours with them. The flours I specify in the ingredient list are those that seem always to work best for my steamed and baked recipes. You may wish to try others; in fact, I urge you to do so.

Most recipes in this chapter, as with virtually all of those in this book, are simple, though some require several steps. That, however, is the way it is with bakers and breadmakers who love the mixing, the kneading, and the rising, all of which eventually give life to dough. Those who enjoy working with dough, who like to have their hands in flour, will enjoy these recipes.

Chicken Won Ton

(Gai Yuk Won Ton)

The varieties of won ton are infinite. Though often regarded as dumplings, they are actually filled noodles, very much like Italian tortellini. Once made, they may be boiled, fried, steamed, or put into soups. They can be eaten as an hors d'oeuvre or a first course, or used as an ingredient, either in soup or by itself at a larger feast. Here is the won ton, in all of its varieties.

For the filling
  1 pound chicken cutlets, ground
  1½ cup finely sliced scallions
  1½ teaspoons minced garlic
  4 fresh water chestnuts, peeled and
    finely diced
  1 tablespoon Chinese white rice
    wine or gin, mixed with
    1½ teaspoons grated ginger
  1 teaspoon salt
  1½ teaspoons sugar
  1 teaspoon light soy sauce

2 teaspoons sesame oil
1 tablespoon oyster sauce
Pinch white pepper
3 tablespoons cornstarch
1 medium egg
1½ tablespoons peanut oil

36 won ton wrappers
3 quarts water
1 tablespoon salt
1 tablespoon peanut oil

In a large bowl combine the filling ingredients and mix well to blend evenly. Place in a shallow dish and refrigerate, uncovered, for 4 hours, or covered overnight.

Make the won ton: The wrappers should be at room temperature. Work with one at a time, keeping the others under a damp towel. Keep a bowl of water at hand to wet the edges of the wrappers. Place a tablespoon of filling in a wrapper, wet the edges, fold the wrapper in half, and seal the edges. Wet the folded corners (not the sealed corners), and draw the ends together to create a bowlike dumpling like a tortellini. Repeat until 36 won ton are made. Place each won ton on a cookie sheet dusted with cornstarch.

Put the water, salt, and peanut oil in a pot, cover, and bring to a boil over high heat. Add the won ton, stir, and cook for about 8 minutes, until they are translucent and the filling can be seen through the wrapper. Turn off the heat. Run cold water into the pot and drain. Repeat and drain well. Place on waxed paper to dry thoroughly.

MAKES 36 WON TON

CHICKEN WITH NOODLES, DUMPLINGS, AND BUNS

*Y*ou *may wish to try some of these variations, each of which uses cooked won ton. If you wish to use all of the won ton in the recipe, do so. If you have some left over, won ton will keep, refrigerated, for up to 4 days or frozen for up to 3 months. If frozen, defrost before use.*

Pan-Fried Won Ton

(JIN WON TON)

Put 3 tablespoons of peanut oil in a frying pan, preferably nonstick. Heat the oil until a wisp of white smoke appears. Add the won ton to the pan and fry on both sides until brown. Turn off the heat and transfer to paper towels to drain. Fry in 2 batches. (You may need to add another tablespoon of peanut oil for second batch.) Serve immediately.

Deep-Fried Won Ton

(JAH WON TON)

Heat a wok over high heat for a minute. Add 5 cups peanut oil and heat to 350° F until boiling. (Oil is at a boil when white smoke rises from it.) Fry the won ton (in two batches if necessary) to a golden brown, turning frequently so they will brown evenly. Turn off the heat. Remove and drain on paper towels. Serve immediately.

Steamed Won Ton

(Jing Won Ton)

Line a steamer with lettuce leaves. Place the won ton in a single layer on the leaves and steam for 5 minutes until very hot. Use one or two steamers, stacked. If the steamers are stacked, add 3 minutes to the steaming time. Turn off the heat. Serve immediately. These are best served right from the steamer. Set the steamer on top of a large platter so any water will drip into it.

All of these won ton recipes may be served with the dipping sauce used for rice paper chicken rolls (page 76), or with a mixture of 2 tablespoons Coleman's dry mustard powder, 2 tablespoons water, and 1½ teaspoons of Tabasco sauce, or to taste.

Won Ton Soup

(WON TON TONG)

You may also use the won ton in soup, perhaps the way most people have eaten them. Bring 4 cups chicken stock (page 36) to a boil and add the won ton, 4 per person. Allow the soup to return to a boil. Add 4 cups shredded lettuce and again bring to a boil. Taste for seasoning. Turn off the heat. Transfer the soup to a pre-heated tureen and serve.

MAKES 4 SERVINGS

Won Ton and Noodle Soup

(WON TON MEIN)

This Cantonese specialty, the most popular variation on the won ton, is very much a classic. As a young girl visiting my aunt in Guangzhou, every evening we would hear the noodle man coming through the streets. He had no need to call out, for we heard him as he clacked bamboo sticks together to announce his arrival. We would race out to the street for bowls of hot won ton and noodles.

2½ cups chicken stock
   (page 36)
6 cups water
16 chicken won ton (page 115)

1 pound fresh Chinese egg noodles
   or size #11 capellini
¼ cup yellow chives cut into
   1½-inch pieces, or garlic chives

Boil the chicken stock and water in separate pots. Add the won ton to the boiling stock, stir, and return to a boil. Turn off the heat. Add the noodles to the boiling water and boil for a minute, stirring to loosen the noodles. Cook the noodles until al dente. Turn off the heat. Run cold water into the pot and drain thoroughly.

Divide the noodles evenly among 4 bowls. Add the soup and 4 won ton to each bowl. Sprinkle with chives and serve.

MAKES 4 SERVINGS

Chicken Lo Mein

(Gai See Lo Mein)

This traditional stir-fried noodle preparation is most familiar to Americans. I expect most, if not all, have had lo mein in a restaurant. It is not, however, often made with the care and with the progression of ingredients necessary to make it the highly regarded dish it ought to be. Once you've made this lo mein with chicken I believe you will be impatient with the careless efforts set forth by some restaurants.

FOR THE SAUCE
- ½ cup chicken stock (page 36)
- 1½ tablespoons Shao-Hsing wine or sherry
- 2 tablespoons oyster sauce
- 2 teaspoons light soy sauce
- 1 teaspoon sesame oil
- Pinch white pepper

- 6 cups cold water
- 1 teaspoon salt
- 8 ounces fresh Chinese egg noodles (as thin as angel hair pasta, which may be substituted)
- 2 tablespoons peanut oil

- 1 teaspoon minced ginger
- 1 teaspoon minced garlic
- 3 steamed black mushrooms (page 42), julienned
- ½ cup carrots cut into 2-inch-long matchsticks
- 2 scallions, trimmed, cut into 2-inch-long sections, white parts quartered lengthwise
- ¼ cup peeled and washed fresh water chestnuts cut into matchsticks
- 4 ounces chicken cutlets, cleaned thoroughly, dried, and cut into 2-inch-long julienne

Put all the sauce ingredients in a bowl and mix well. Reserve.

Put the cold water in a large pot and add the salt. Cover and bring to a boil over high heat. Add the noodles, loosening them with chopsticks, and cook for 1½ minutes or until al dente. Turn off the heat. Run cold water into the pot and drain. Repeat twice more and drain thoroughly. Reserve.

Heat a wok over high heat for 30 seconds. Add the peanut oil and coat the wok with it, using a spatula. When a wisp of white smoke appears, add the ginger and garlic and stir briefly. Add all the vegetables and stir-fry together for 2½ minutes. Turn off the heat, remove the vegetables, and reserve.

Stir the reserved sauce and pour it into the wok. Turn the heat back on to high.

Add the chicken and stir to separate while allowing the sauce to come to a boil. Add the reserved vegetables and stir. Add the reserved noodles, mix well, and cook until all the liquid has been absorbed. Turn off the heat. Transfer the mixture to a preheated dish, and serve.

MAKES 4 SERVINGS

Double-Fried Noodles with Chicken

(Gai See Chau Mein)

This traditional noodle dish from Shanghai is called leung mein wong, *which translates as "yellow both sides." The noodles are fried twice, once on each side, to a golden color; they are also often deep-fried until crisp throughout. I prefer this version from Shanghai, also quite popular in Hong Kong, in which the noodles are crisp on the surface but soft inside. Though it can be made with various foods atop the noodles chicken is the preferred ingredient.*

2 quarts water
2 teaspoons salt
8 ounces fresh Chinese egg noodles, fine (or #11 capellini)

FOR THE SAUCE
1 tablespoon light soy sauce
1¼ teaspoons sugar
1 teaspoon sesame oil
1 tablespoon Shao-Hsing wine or sherry
Pinch white pepper
2½ teaspoons cornstarch
⅔ cup chicken stock (page 36)

4½ tablespoons peanut oil
1 teaspoon minced ginger
1 teaspoon minced garlic
4 ounces chicken cutlet, cleaned thoroughly, dried, julienned, and marinated for 20 minutes in
1 teaspoon sesame oil
¼ cup julienned bamboo shoots
3 scallions, trimmed and cut into 2-inch-long pieces, white portions julienned
3 steamed black mushrooms (page 42), julienned

Combine the water and salt in a pot, cover, and bring to a boil over high heat. Add the noodles, stir, and cook for a minute. Turn off the heat. Run cold water into the pot and drain. Rinse again and then allow the noodles to drain for 2 hours, turning occasionally until completely dry. Mix the sauce ingredients and reserve.

Heat a cast-iron skillet over high heat for 40 seconds and add 2 tablespoons of the peanut oil. When a wisp of white smoke appears, place the noodles in the skillet in an even layer, covering the entire bottom. Lower the heat to medium, fry for 2 minutes, then fry for 3 minutes more, moving the pan from side to side to ensure the noodles brown evenly and do not stick. Turn off the heat. Slide the noodles onto a large flat dish and invert another dish over it. Turn the dish over and slide the noodles back into skillet. (The fried side is now on top.) Turn the heat to medium and repeat the frying. If a bit more oil is needed, add it, but only if absolutely necessary.

While the noodles cook, heat a wok over high heat for 40 seconds and add 1½ tablespoons of the peanut oil. Coat the wok with it, using a spatula. When a wisp of white smoke appears, add the ginger and garlic and stir briefly. Add the chicken, spread it in a thin layer, and cook for a minute. Turn the chicken over and mix well. Add the vegetables and stir-fry with the chicken for 2 minutes. Make a well in the mixture, stir the reserved sauce and pour it in. Stir until the sauce thickens and bubbles. Turn off the heat.

Assemble the dish by placing the fried noodles on a preheated platter. Pour the contents of the wok over the noodles. Cut the mixture into 4 wedge-shaped pieces and serve immediately.

MAKES 4 SERVINGS

NOTE: The noodles may be boiled the night before, allowed to dry, then refrigerated to save time. In that case, the noodles should be allowed to return to room temperature before frying; otherwise, the cooking time will be longer.

Lemon Noodles with Chicken

(Ling Mung Gai Mein)

The use of lemon and other citrus fruits in cooking is common in southern China, particularly in the Guangdong region, where they grow in profusion. In general, the cooks of Canton use whole fruits and whole dried fruit skins. Seldom is fresh rind used in classic cookery. This recipe is my design. I have borrowed the use of grated lemon zest from the West and added it to an essentially Chinese preparation.

8 ounces dried rice noodles
3 tablespoons scallion oil (page 38)
1½ teaspoons minced garlic
¾ teaspoon salt
1½ teaspoons sugar
1 teaspoon grated lemon zest

1 cup roasted chicken (page 60) cut
   into 2-inch-long julienne
1 tablespoon fresh lemon juice
   mixed with 1½ tablespoons
   Tabasco sauce
1 scallion, trimmed and finely sliced

Soak the rice noodles in hot water for 20 minutes. Drain through a strainer, loosen and allow to dry.

Heat a wok over high heat for 30 seconds. Add the scallion oil, garlic, salt, and sugar and stir together briefly. Add the lemon zest and stir. Add the chicken and stir for a minute. Add the noodles, lower the heat, and mix all the ingredients thoroughly. Cook for 2 minutes. Add the lemon juice–Tabasco mixture and toss. When the noodles are well mixed and coated, turn off the heat and add the scallions. Mix well. Transfer the mixture to a preheated platter and serve immediately.

MAKES 4 SERVINGS

Sesame Noodles with Chicken

(Chi Ma Gai Mein)

This, too, is a recipe I have designed. It is a simple combination of three ingredients: chicken, fresh noodles, and roasted sesame seeds, but the taste that emerges from this blending is surprisingly complex.

FOR THE SAUCE
- 1½ tablespoons dark soy sauce
- 1½ tablespoons light soy sauce
- 2 tablespoons oyster sauce
- 2 teaspoons Chinese white rice vinegar or distilled white vinegar
- 1½ teaspoons sesame oil
- 3 tablespoons chicken stock (page 36)
- 1 tablespoon sugar
- ¼ teaspoon salt
- Pinch white pepper

- 1 tablespoon white sesame seeds
- 10 cups water
- 2 teaspoons salt
- 1 pound fresh Chinese egg noodles (or linguine)
- 2½ tablespoons white peppercorn oil (page 39)
- 1½ teaspoons minced ginger
- 1½ teaspoons minced garlic
- 1½ cups roasted chicken meat (page 60) cut into 2½-inch-long by ¼-inch-wide julienne
- 3 tablespoons finely sliced scallions

Mix the sauce ingredients in a bowl and reserve. Dry-roast the sesame seeds over low heat for a minute (see page 16) and reserve.

Put the water and salt in a large pot, cover, and bring to a boil over high heat. Add the noodles and cook for 1½ minutes, stirring and loosening, until al dente. Turn off the heat. Run cold water into the pot, and drain the noodles through a strainer. Put the noodles back in the pot and fill with cold water. Mix the noodles with your hands and drain them again through a strainer to remove excess starch. Allow to drain for 3 minutes, loosening the noodles with chopsticks.

Heat a wok over high heat for 30 seconds, add the oil, and coat the wok with it, using a spatula. When a wisp of white smoke appears, add the ginger and garlic and stir briefly. Add the chicken and stir and cook for a minute. Stir the reserved sauce and pour it in, stirring and mixing until it bubbles. Add the noodles and toss well. Lower the heat and cook until the sauce is absorbed by the noodles, 1½ to 2 minutes. Turn off the heat, add the reserved sesame seeds, and toss well. Transfer the mixture to a preheated platter, sprinkle with scallions, and serve.

MAKES 4 TO 6 SERVINGS

Singapore Noodles

(Sing Jau Gai See Chau Mai Fan)

This is a classic from Southeast Asia, particularly Singapore, where it was born, but it has become a standard in China and in Chinese restaurants around the world. Although it is traditionally made with barbecued pork, chicken is often used as well, particularly among the Moslems in Singapore, who do not eat pork. We have them to thank for this fine variation of a classic dish.

8 ounces dry rice noodles

FOR THE SAUCE
2 teaspoons light soy sauce
2½ tablespoons oyster sauce
2 teaspoons sugar
½ teaspoon salt
¼ cup chicken stock
　(page 36)

FOR THE CURRY MIXTURE
2 tablespoons curry powder
¼ teaspoon cayenne pepper,
　optional
2½ tablespoons chicken stock

1 quart cold water
¼ pound bean sprouts, washed and
　drained
2½ tablespoons peanut oil
2 teaspoons minced ginger
½ teaspoon salt
1 cup roasted chicken (page 60) cut
　into julienne 2 inches long by
　¼ inch wide
3 tablespoons chicken stock
4 scallions, trimmed, cut into
　1½-inch-long pieces, white parts
　quartered lengthwise
2 fresh water chestnuts, peeled,
　washed, and julienned
½ large red bell pepper, julienned
　(½ cup)

Soak the rice noodles in hot water for 20 minutes until softened. Drain, toss by hand to remove all water, and reserve. Mix the sauce in a bowl and reserve. In a separate bowl, combine the curry mixture ingredients and set aside.

In a large pot, bring the water to a boil over high heat. Blanch the bean sprouts in water for 8 seconds. Turn off the heat. Run cold water into the pot and drain. Rinse with cold water and drain again. Reserve.

Heat a wok over high heat for 30 seconds, add the peanut oil, and coat the wok with it, using a spatula. When a wisp of white smoke appears, add the ginger and salt and stir for 15 seconds. Add the curry mixture. Cook for 30 seconds until its aroma is released. Add the chicken and stir briefly. Add the chicken stock and stir and cook for a minute. Add the scallions and stir. Make a well in the mixture, stir the reserved sauce, and pour it in. Mix thoroughly. Add the reserved noodles and toss until they are well coated and become yellow from the curry. Add the water chestnuts and bean sprouts and stir for a minute. Add the bell peppers and mix well for 2 minutes until the noodles are very hot. Turn off the heat. Transfer to a preheated platter and serve.

MAKES 4 SERVINGS

Fresh Rice Noodles
with Chicken and Black Beans

(See Jiu Gai Chau Hor)

This snowy white noodle, sold in sheets already cooked by steaming, is a favorite not only in teahouses and noodle shops but in restaurants as well, where it is usually folded around fillings. But this noodle is not limited to steaming. Cut up, it finds its way into soups; cut into recognizable noodle shapes and stir-fried with chicken and pungent fermented black beans, is most satisfying.

FOR THE MARINADE
- 1 tablespoon light soy sauce
- 1 tablespoon sesame oil
- 1½ teaspoons salt
- 2½ teaspoons sugar
- ½ teaspoon ginger juice mixed with 2 teaspoons Chinese white rice wine or gin
- 2½ tablespoons oyster sauce
- 2 teaspoons cornstarch
- Pinch white pepper

- 6 ounces chicken cutlet, cleaned thoroughly, dried, and sliced into pieces 2½ inches long by ¼ inch wide
- 2½ tablespoons peanut oil
- 1 slice ginger, ½ inch thick, lightly smashed
- 1 tablespoons minced garlic
- 2 tablespoons fermented black beans, rinsed twice and drained
- ¾ cup thinly sliced red bell pepper
- ¾ cup thinly sliced green bell pepper
- 1 pound fresh rice noodles, cut into pieces 2 inches long by ¾ inch wide

Combine the marinade ingredients in a large bowl, add the chicken, and toss gently. Allow to rest for 20 minutes.

Heat a wok over high heat for 30 seconds. Add 1½ tablespoons of the peanut oil and coat the wok with it, using a spatula. When a wisp of white smoke appears, add the ginger and stir briefly. Add the garlic and black beans and stir until their fragrance is released, about a minute. Add the chicken and marinade and spread in a thin layer. Cook for 30 seconds and turn over. Add the bell peppers and stir for 30 seconds. Add the rice noodles and stir well. (If the dish is too dry, add the remaining tablespoon of peanut oil.) Cook for 3 to 4 minutes, until the mixture is very hot. Turn off the heat. Transfer to a preheated platter and serve immediately.

MAKES 4 TO 6 SERVINGS

Ginger Noodles with Chicken

(GEUNG SEE GAI MEIN)

This noodle dish emphasizes the fine tastes of fresh ginger, particularly the young, smooth ginger of spring, summer, and fall, a taste that is subtle and less spicy than older ginger root. When fresh ginger is available, which is most of the year in southern China, the Chinese always demand that these noodles be made with ji geung, *or "baby boy ginger," which complements chicken so well.*

FOR THE SAUCE
2½ tablespoons oyster sauce
2 teaspoons light soy sauce
1 teaspoon sugar
4 tablespoons chicken stock
   (page 36)
1½ teaspoons sesame seed oil
Pinch white pepper

8 cups cold water
2 teaspoons salt
8 ounces fresh Chinese egg noodles
   (or linguine)

2½ tablespoons peanut oil
4 tablespoons fresh young ginger,
   shredded (if unavailable,
   use 3 tablespoons regular
   ginger)
1 cup poached chicken (page 61) cut
   into 2-inch-long
   julienne
1 cup scallions cut into
   1½-inch-long pieces, white parts
   of 4 to 6 scallions quartered
   lengthwise

Combine the sauce ingredients in a bowl and reserve.

Put the water and salt in a large pot, cover, and bring to a boil over high heat. Add the noodles and stir and cook for a minute, or until al dente. Turn off the heat. Run cold water into the pot and drain the noodles through a strainer. Put the noodles back in the pot and fill the pot with cold water. Mix the noodles with your hands and drain through a strainer. Repeat. (This removes excess starch from the noodles.) Allow the noodles to drain for 10 to 15 minutes, loosening them with your hands. Reserve.

Heat a wok over high heat for 45 seconds. Add the peanut oil and coat the wok with it, using a spatula. When a wisp of white smoke appears, add the ginger and stir-fry for 30 seconds. Add the noodles and mix with the ginger until the noodles are very hot. Add the chicken and scallions, mix well, and cook for 2 minutes. Make a well in the mixture, stir the reserved sauce and pour it in. Stir and cook for

2 minutes, making certain that the chicken and noodles are well coated and that the liquid is absorbed. Turn off the heat. Transfer to a preheated platter and serve immediately.

MAKES 4 SERVINGS

Steamed Chicken Buns

(Jing Gai Bau)

The steamed buns with which most people are familiar are usually filled with seasoned cooked pork, vegetables, or sweet lotus seed or bean pastes. A more elegant, more delicate bun filling is chicken, found in the teahouses of Canton and Hong Kong. In these teahouses chicken is a happy combination with lighter teas.

This recipe, as well as the two that follow, are particularly recommended for those who love to work with dough and who love to bake and make breads. These buns and breads are truly worth the effort.

FOR THE MARINADE
1 teaspoon light soy sauce
1/2 teaspoon sesame oil
1/4 teaspoon grated ginger mixed
   with 1/2 teaspoon Shao-Hsing
   wine or sherry
1/2 teaspoon sugar
1 1/2 teaspoons oyster sauce
Pinch white pepper
3/4 teaspoon cornstarch

4 ounces chicken cutlet, cleaned,
   dried, and cut into 1/3-inch cubes

FOR THE SAUCE
1 tablespoon oyster sauce
1/4 teaspoon light soy sauce
1/4 teaspoon dark soy sauce
1/2 teaspoon sesame oil

1/2 teaspoon sugar
1/8 teaspoon salt
2 teaspoons tapioca starch
Pinch white pepper
3 tablespoons chicken stock
   (page 36)

1 tablespoon peanut oil
1/4 cup dried black mushrooms,
   soaked in warm water for
   30 minutes, stems removed, and
   cut into 1/4-inch pieces
1 tablespoon bamboo shoots cut
   into 1/4-inch pieces
1 1/2 teaspoons Shao-Hsing wine or
   sherry
1 scallion, white part only, minced
   (1/8 cup)

Prepare the filling: Combine the marinade ingredients in a bowl, add the chicken, and marinate for 30 minutes. Combine the sauce ingredients in a separate bowl and reserve.

Heat a wok over high heat for 30 seconds. Add the peanut oil and coat the wok with it, using a spatula. When a wisp of white smoke appears, add the chicken and marinade in a thin layer, and cook for 30 seconds. Turn the chicken mixture over and mix. Add the mushrooms and bamboo shoots and stir and cook for a minute. Add the wine by drizzling it in from the edge of the wok and mix well. Add the scallions and stir-fry for 30 seconds. Make a well in the center of the mixture, stir the reserved sauce and pour it in. Stir well, cooking until the sauce thickens and bubbles. Turn off the heat. Transfer the mixture to a shallow dish and allow to come to room temperature. (You may refrigerate for 4 hours uncovered or overnight, covered.)

While the filling rests, make the dough (recipe follows).

Prepare the buns: cut out eight 2½-inch squares of waxed paper. Reserve. Roll the dough into a cylinder 8 inches long and cut it into eight 1-inch sections. Roll each piece into a ball. Work with one piece at a time and cover the remaining pieces with a damp cloth. Press the ball of dough down lightly and then, using your fingers, press the dough into a domelike shape open at the top. Place a tablespoon of filling in the center of the well that has been formed, close the dome, and pleat with fingers until completely closed.

Place the bun on a square of waxed paper, pleated side up. Repeat until all 8 buns are made. Place the buns in a steamer at least 2 inches apart to allow for expansion. Steam for 15 to 20 minutes until pleated upper sides open like flowers. The buns are now done. Serve immediately.

MAKES 8 STEAMED BUNS

NOTES: Use only a tablespoon of filling initially, until you have learned to work with the dough. Otherwise you will have difficulty sealing the bun. When you feel more comfortable working with the dough, increase the amount of filling to 2 tablespoons.

Buns may be frozen after steaming and will keep in the freezer for 2 to 3 months. To reheat, defrost thoroughly and steam for 5 minutes.

This recipe may be doubled to yield 16 buns, if desired.

Steamed Bun Dough

1¼ cups flour (preferably Gold
    Medal All-Purpose, enriched and
    bleached)
1¾ teaspoons baking powder

¼ cup sugar
3 tablespoons milk
2 tablespoons water
1½ tablespoons peanut oil

Mix the flour, baking powder, and sugar together on a work surface. Make a well in the center of the mixture, add the milk, and combine with your fingers. After the milk has been absorbed, add the water and with your fingers continue to work the dough. Add the peanut oil and continue to work the dough.

Using a dough scraper, gather the dough in one hand and begin kneading with the other. Knead for 10 minutes. If the dough is dry, sprinkle it with water and continue to knead, until the dough become elastic. If the dough is wet, sprinkle a bit of flour on the work surface and on your hands and continue working. When the dough is elastic, cover it with a damp cloth and allow to rest for an hour. The dough is then ready to use.

Baked Chicken Buns

(Guk Gai Bau)

Baked buns are almost always filled with seasoned roast pork. This is my varia-tion: I use stir-fried and seasoned chicken for the filling, an adaptation that has delighted my family. As you will note, the basic filling ingredients are similar to those in the previous steamed bun recipe. I have deliberately chosen the two recipes to demonstrate how different the results can be between steamed and baked buns, and between doughs of different ingredients and consistencies.

I prefer eating these buns without accompaniment. My family, however, likes them with a hot mustard sauce of equal amounts of Coleman's mustard powder and water, and Tabasco sauce to taste.

1 recipe filling from steamed
    chicken buns (page 131; see steps
    in paragraphs 1 and 2 of the
    instructions)

FOR THE BAKED BUN DOUGH
    1½ teaspoons dry yeast
    5 tablespoons sugar
    ⅓ cup hot water

1⅓ cups high gluten flour
    (preferably Pillsbury Best Bread
    Flour, enriched, bromide)
1 small egg, beaten
3¾ tablespoons peanut oil
1 small egg, beaten, for egg wash
2 tablespoons scallion oil (page 38)
    for brushing

Make the chicken bun filling. While it rests, make the dough: In a large mixing bowl, dissolve the yeast and sugar in hot water. Set in a warm place for 30 to 60 minutes, depending upon the outside temperature. (In winter, the longer time will be required.)

When the yeast rises and a brownish foam forms on top, add the flour, beaten egg, and peanut oil, stirring continuously with your hand. Begin kneading. When the dough becomes cohesive, sprinkle a work surface with flour, place the dough on it, and continue kneading. Knead for about 15 minutes, picking up the dough with a scraper and sprinkling the work surface with flour to prevent sticking. When the dough is smooth and elastic, place it in a large bowl. Cover with a damp cloth and place in a warm place to rise. The dough will take from 2 to 4 hours to rise, depending on the temperature (it will take longer in cold weather). The dough is ready when it has tripled in size.

Prepare the buns: Cut out eight 3½-inch squares of waxed paper. Reserve.

Remove the dough from the bowl, knead it several times, and then roll it out with your hands into a sausage shape, 8 inches long. Divide into eight 1-inch pieces. Work with one piece at a time, keeping the remaining dough under a damp cloth. Roll each piece into a ball, and using your fingers, press each one to create a well. Place a tablespoon of filling into the well that has been created. Hold the bun in one hand and with the other turn the bun, pinching it closed. Press firmly to seal. (As your proficiency with the dough grows, increase the filling to 2 tablespoons.) Place the completed bun, sealed side down, on a square of waxed paper. Repeat until all the buns are made.

Place the buns on a cookie sheet at least 2 inches apart to allow for expansion. Place in a warm spot for about an hour to rise. (The rising time will be longer in winter.) Preheat the oven to 350° F for 20 minutes. Using an atomizer, spray each bun lightly with warm water. With a pastry brush, brush each bun with beaten egg. Bake for 15 to 20 minutes. Halfway through the baking time, rotate the cookie sheet. When the buns are golden brown, remove from the oven, turn off the heat, and while still warm, brush with scallion oil. (As the buns cool, the crust tends to harden slightly. The oil prevents hardening, as well as adding flavor.) Serve immediately.

MAKES 8 BAKED BUNS

NOTE: I prefer not to freeze buns, since they tend to dry out. They will keep, refrigerated, for 3 or 4 days. When reheating, allow to come to room temperature, sprinkle lightly with water, and heat in a 350° F oven for 5 minutes.

This recipe, like that for steamed buns, can be doubled.

Steamed Lotus Leaf Breads

(Haw Yip Bang)

These small steamed breads, shaped like rounded lotus leaves, are the basic steamed breads of Beijing, where they are eaten widely with a variety of dishes, quite like Westerners eat bread. They are also enjoyed in Sichuan, Hunan, and Hong Kong.

These delicate steamed breads can accompany many of the dishes in this book. In particular I recommend serving them with Cantonese Fried Chicken (page 53), Viceroy's Chicken (page 184), Lion's Heads (page 201), Roasted Chicken (page 60), Cinnamon-Scented Chicken (page 57), Twice-Fried String Beans with Minced Chicken (page 189), Eight-Piece Chicken (page 193), and Chicken with Leeks, Beijing Style (page 182).

1 cup Pillsbury Best All-Purpose Flour, enriched, bleached
¼ cup Pillsbury Best Bread Flour, enriched, bromide
¼ cup sugar
2 teaspoons baking powder
¼ cup lukewarm milk
⅛ cup lukewarm water
1¼ tablespoons lard or peanut oil
Thirty 2-inch squares parchment

Mix the flours, sugar, and baking powder together on a work surface. Make a well in the middle, add the milk gradually, and combine the dough with your fingers. After the milk has been absorbed, add the water and continue to work the dough with your fingers. Add the lard (or peanut oil) and using your fingers continue to work the dough until well blended. Knead the dough into an elastic ball and allow to rest for an hour.

Divide the dough in half. Roll each half into a cylinder 15 inches long. Cut each cylinder into 1-inch pieces. Work with one piece at a time, keeping the remaining dough covered with a damp cloth. Roll each piece into a ball. Press it down on the work surface with your palm into a round 1½ inches in diameter. Retain the round shape but pinch the bottom of each piece to make a small protrusion.

After pressing, the dough will widen at the sides into the desired lotus leaf shape. Press a dinner fork into the dough to create fanlike lines and ridges. If the dough is too moist, dust with flour. Place each piece on a square of parchment or waxed paper. Repeat until 30 small lotus leaf breads have been formed. Place the breads in a steamer (10 to a steamer), cover, and steam for 10 minutes. Turn off the heat. Remove the breads and serve hot.

MAKES 30 SMALL BREADS

NOTE: After steaming, these breads may be kept, covered with plastic wrap, for 3 days in the refrigerator. They may also be frozen. Bring to room temperature before steaming again.

Dumplings

Most Westerners were introduced to the Chinese dumpling in dim sum restaurants. For many, Sunday morning dim sum at their favorite Chinese restaurants is a recurrent weekly joy. The dumpling—a light, often transparent dough enclosing a savory or sweet filling either steamed, boiled, or fried—is one of the joys of Chinese cooking.

Small half-moon chicken pastries, tiny steamed baskets of seasoned meats, seafood and chicken, steamed triangles and crescents of stuffed bean curd, small pillows filled with shrimp or chicken and fish, horns, rolls, cylinders, balls and envelopes of dough: the tastes, shapes, and textures of the Chinese dumpling are endless.

The dumpling had its beginnings during the years of the Song dynasty, according to some historians, when tenth-century travelers along the roads and trade routes of southern China began stopping for tea and small foods at roadside teahouses. In some of these teahouses the small foods and snacks became the focus of their establishments, and the dim sum teahouse, the dim sum parlor, and the dim sum restaurant came into being. These days, in cities such as Hong Kong, Guangzhou, Shanghai, and Beijing, the dumpling crosses regional lines, and it is said that a master dumpling chef will have hundreds of dim sum in his repertoire.

I have written extensively of dim sum and dumplings and shall never tire of doing so, nor will I ever grow weary of fashioning these little culinary objects of art, cooking them, and feeding them to my family and guests. Particularly at our family's Christmas celebration, we eat dumplings by the hundreds along with Champagne. What follows is a small collection of classic chicken dumplings that I am certain you will delight in making and even more in serving. The recipes for each of the four dumplings that follow will serve 4 to 6; the recipes may be doubled successfully.

All of the dumplings in this chapter will keep refrigerated for 2 to 3 days. They may be frozen. If you plan to freeze them for future use, undercook them by 2 minutes, drain, and dry well before freezing. To recook the Chicken Water Dumplings, the Chicken Siu Mai, and the Chive and Chicken Dumplings, defrost thoroughly, then steam for 3 to 4 minutes. They may also be heated in boiling water for 2 minutes. To recook the street dumplings, defrost and pan-fry for 2 minutes.

Chicken Water Dumplings

(Gai Yuk Soi Gau)

These dumplings are aptly named because they are cooked completely, or partially, in boiling water. In a teahouse, a water dumpling might be boiled partially and then finished in individual steamers for serving. There is, however, no need for this extra process; boiled water dumplings are sufficiently tasty.

4 cups cold water
½ teaspoon salt
¾ cup Tianjin bok choy stems and
   2 cups of leaves cut into
   ½-inch-long pieces, tightly
   packed to yield 8 ounces
8 ounces chicken cutlet, cleaned
   thoroughly, dried, and coarsely
   ground
2 teaspoons sesame oil
2 scallions, trimmed and finely
   sliced
½ teaspoon ginger juice mixed with
   1 teaspoon Shao-Hsing wine or
   sherry

1½ tablespoons oyster sauce
1 teaspoon light soy sauce
1¼ teaspoons sugar
¼ teaspoon salt
Pinch white pepper
1½ tablespoons cornstarch

24 dumpling wrappers

FOR THE BOILING
2 quarts cold water
1 teaspoon salt
1 tablespoon peanut oil

Water-blanch the bok choy: Put the water and salt in a pot, cover, and bring to a boil over high heat. Add the stems, stir, and cook for 30 seconds. Add the leaves and allow the water to return to a boil, about a minute. Turn off the heat. Run cold water into the pot. Drain thoroughly and reserve.

In a large bowl combine the reserved bok choy and remaining ingredients (except the dumpling wrappers and boiling ingredients) and mix thoroughly until well blended. Place the mixture in a shallow dish, and refrigerate uncovered for 4 hours or overnight, covered.

Make the dumplings: The wrappers should be at room temperature. When working with the wrappers keep those not in use covered with a damp cloth. With kitchen shears, cut the dumpling skins into rounds 3 inches in diameter. Place a tablespoon of filling in the center of a skin and wet the edges with water. Fold the wrapper into a half moon and press together tightly along the curved edge with thumb and forefinger to seal. Repeat until all the dumplings are made.

Cook the dumplings: Put the boiling ingredients in a large pot, cover, and bring to a boil over high heat. Add the dumplings and boil for 5 to 6 minutes until done. (The dumplings will change color and float to the top of the water when done.) Turn off the heat. Run cold water into the pot and drain. Serve immediately.

MAKES 24 WATER DUMPLINGS

Chicken Siu Mai

(GAI YUK SIU MAI)

Siu mai, or "cook and sell" dumplings, are traditions of the Chinese teahouse, their name called out in a sing-song voice by the women who push the dim sum carts. They are called "cook and sell" because they are siu, or made, then mai, or sold, quickly. Most commonly filled with a mixture of pork and shrimp, they are quite elegant when filled with chicken.

10 ounces chicken cutlet, cleaned thoroughly, dried, and coarsely ground
⅓ cup fresh peeled and washed water chestnuts cut into ⅛-inch dice
⅓ cup bamboo shoots cut into ⅛-inch dice
⅓ cup finely sliced scallions
1 tablespoon minced ginger
1 tablespoon Shao-Hsing wine or sherry

¼ teaspoon salt
1½ teaspoons sugar
1 teaspoon light soy sauce
1½ tablespoons oyster sauce
2 tablespoons white peppercorn oil (page 39)
2½ tablespoons cornstarch
1 teaspoon sesame oil
Pinch white pepper
1 large egg white, beaten
24 dumpling wrappers

Make the filling: Combine the chicken and all the other ingredients except the wrappers and mix thoroughly. Place the mixture in a shallow dish and refrigerate uncovered for 4 hours or overnight, covered.

Make the dumplings: Work with one wrapper at a time and keep those not in use covered with a damp cloth. With kitchen shears cut each wrapper into a 2½-inch round. Place 1½ tablespoons filling in the center of a wrapper. Hold the filling in place with the blade of a butter knife in one hand and, holding the dumpling in the other, gradually turn the knife and dumpling slowly in the same direction so that the dumpling forms a basket shape.

Remove the knife, pack down the filling and smooth. Squeeze the dumpling slightly to create a "neck" so that the dumpling and filling will remain intact during the steaming process. Tap the dumpling bottom lightly on the work surface to flatten. Place the dumplings on their bottoms in an oil-brushed steamer and steam for 6 minutes until done. Turn off the heat. Remove the steamer from the wok and place it on a platter. Serve the dumplings directly from the steamer.

MAKES 24 DUMPLINGS

CHICKEN WITH NOODLES, DUMPLINGS, AND BUNS

Chive and Chicken Dumplings

(Gai Yuk Gau Choi Gau)

Making dumplings containing chives along with other ingredients is a long tradition of the Chiu Chow people of southern China. Over the years they have become standards in the dim sum repertoire. A pleasurable part of dumpling making is the variety of shapes available. This dumpling, with a traditional filling of chicken and fresh garlic chives, is shaped like a cockscomb, a favorite shape in the teahouses of Hong Kong.

1½ tablespoons white peppercorn oil (page 39)
½ teaspoon salt
1 tablespoon minced ginger
8 ounces garlic chives, washed to remove grit, dried, and cut into ⅓-inch-long pieces
8 ounces chicken meat, preferably leg meat, cleaned thoroughly, dried, and ground
1½ teaspoons light soy sauce
2½ teaspoons Shao-Hsing wine or sherry
2 teaspoons sugar

2 tablespoons oyster sauce
1½ teaspoons sesame oil
Pinch white pepper
2½ tablespoons cornstarch

24 dumpling wrappers

FOR THE BOILING
2 quarts cold water
1 tablespoon salt
1 tablespoon peanut oil

Ginger soy sauce dip (recipe follows)

Heat a wok over high heat for 30 seconds. Add the oil and coat the wok with it, using a spatula. When a wisp of white smoke appears, add the salt and ginger and stir briefly. Add the chives and stir-fry for 1½ minutes until they turn bright green. Turn off the heat. Transfer the chives to a mesh strainer and drain over a bowl. Loosen the chives with a fork to help them drain and allow to cool.

In a bowl put the chicken, chives, and soy sauce, wine, sugar, oyster sauce, sesame oil, pepper, and cornstarch and mix well. Place the mixture in a shallow dish and refrigerate uncovered for 4 hours, or covered, overnight.

Make the dumplings: Work with one wrapper at a time and cover those not in use with a damp cloth. With kitchen shears cut the wrappers into 3¼-inch rounds. Place a tablespoon of filling in the center of the wrapper. Use a butter knife to press the filling down, and with the knife moisten the entire edge of the wrapper with water. Fold the wrapper into a half moon and press the edges together with thumb and forefinger to seal. Using the butter knife, moisten both sides of the pressed edge with water. Gradually, beginning at one end, fold the curved edge into a series of small overlaps to create the "crest" of the cockscomb. Press to retain this shape. Repeat until 24 dumplings are made. Place the dumplings on a flour-dusted cookie sheet to prevent sticking.

Cook the dumplings: Put the boiling ingredients in a large pot, cover, and bring to a boil over high heat. Add the dumplings and stir to prevent sticking. Allow to return to a boil. Boil the dumplings for 5 minutes or until they are cooked through. Turn off the heat. Run cold water over the dumplings and drain. Serve immediately with individual dishes of ginger soy sauce dip.

MAKES 24 DUMPLINGS

Ginger Soy Sauce Dip

3 tablespoons light soy sauce
4 tablespoons chicken stock
  (page 36)

2 tablespoons minced ginger
2 teaspoons sesame oil

Mix all the ingredients together in a bowl.

MAKES 4 SMALL SERVINGS

Street Dumplings

(GAI BIN GAU)

These very special dumplings have a bit of modern history attached to them. They were created by the refugees from Shanghai who fled their city in the 1950s revolution and came to Hong Kong. They would set up portable charcoal or coal stoves in the streets and make these dumplings for people to lunch on. Later, many of these entrepreneurs went on to open restaurants. These dumplings have remained popular up to today.

12 ounces chicken meat, preferably leg meat, cleaned thoroughly, dried, and ground

⅓ cup celery (tender inside stalks only) cut into ⅛-inch dice

3 scallions, trimmed and finely sliced

1 tablespoon minced ginger

1 tablespoon sesame oil

1½ teaspoons Chinese white rice vinegar or distilled vinegar

2 teaspoons sugar

¾ teaspoon salt

1½ tablespoons oyster sauce

Pinch white pepper

1½ tablespoons cornstarch

16 square won ton wrappers

4 tablespoons peanut oil

⅔ cup cold water

Vinegar ginger dip (recipe follows)

Make the filling: Combine all the ingredients except the wrappers, peanut oil, and cold water and mix well. Place in a shallow dish and refrigerate uncovered for 4 hours, or overnight, covered.

Make the dumplings: Work with one wrapper at a time and cover those not in use with a damp cloth. Place a tablespoon of filling in the center of the wrapper. Use a butter knife to wet the edges of the wrapper. Pick up two opposite corners, bring them together, and squeeze to seal and create a triangle. Pick up the other two opposite corners and squeeze them together with the first two. This will create a knoblike shape. Twist the dough at the point of closure. Turn the dumpling over and shape it into a round bundle, sealed side down. Repeat until all the dumplings are formed.

Fry the dumplings: For each batch of 8, heat 2 tablespoons of the peanut oil in a large, cast-iron skillet over high heat until a wisp of white smoke appears. Place 8 dumplings in the skillet and cook for 2 minutes. Pour ⅓ cup of cold water into the skillet, cover, reduce the heat to medium, and cook until all the water has evaporated. Uncover, reduce the heat to low, and continue to cook, rotating the skillet to distribute the heat evenly, until the dumplings are golden brown on the bottom and somewhat translucent on top (1 to 2 minutes longer). Remove from the skillet and drain on paper towels. Repeat with second batch using the remaining 2 tablespoons of peanut oil and water. Serve immediately with vinegar ginger dip.

MAKES 16 DUMPLINGS

Vinegar Ginger Dip

2 tablespoons red wine vinegar
6 tablespoons water
2 tablespoons double dark soy sauce

2 teaspoons sugar
4 tablespoons shredded ginger

In a small bowl, combine all the ingredients and mix well. Allow the mixture to stand for an hour and then divide among small condiment plates for dipping.

MAKES ENOUGH FOR 4 SMALL SERVINGS

Chicken Spring Rolls

(GAI SEE CHUN GEUN)

Perhaps no food preparation in the Chinese repertoire is more familiar than the spring roll. Who does not know of the spring roll or has not eaten at least one? Nothing has been borrowed more or altered more from Chinese cooking. We have all had so-called spring rolls filled with everything from head cheese to raspberries and everything in between, so enamored are today's chefs with the spring roll. The spring roll is indeed a Chinese delicacy, delicate, finger-like, filled with the foods of spring, from which its name derives.

FOR THE SAUCE
- 2 teaspoons light soy sauce
- ¼ teaspoon salt
- 1 teaspoon sugar
- 1 teaspoon sesame oil
- 2 teaspoons Shao-Hsing wine or sherry
- 2½ tablespoons cornstarch
- ⅓ cup chicken stock (page 36)
- Pinch white pepper

- 5 cups cold water
- 1 teaspoon salt
- 8 ounces Tianjin bok choy leaves, cut lengthwise and then into ¼-inch-wide slices, tightly packed to yield 4 cups
- 1½ tablespoons plus 5 cups peanut oil
- 6 ounces chicken cutlet, cleaned thoroughly, dried, and cut into 2-inch-long julienne
- 16 spring roll wrappers
- 2 large eggs, beaten

Combine the sauce ingredients in a bowl and reserve

Put the cold water and salt in a pot, cover, and bring to a boil over high heat. Water-blanch the bok choy: Add the bok choy to the pot, stir, and cook for 40 seconds. Turn off the heat. Run cold water into the pot and drain. Repeat. Allow the bok choy to drain through a strainer for 20 minutes, loosening occasionally. Reserve.

Prepare the filling: Heat a wok over high heat for 30 seconds. Add the 1½ tablespoons peanut oil and coat the wok with it, using a spatula. When a wisp of white smoke appears, add the chicken. Spread it in a thin layer and cook for 30 seconds. Turn the chicken over and mix. Add the bok choy, mix well, and cook for a minute. Make a well in the center of the mixture, stir the reserved sauce and pour it in. Mix well until the sauce bubbles and thickens. Turn off the heat. Transfer to a shallow dish. Refrigerate uncovered for 4 hours, or overnight, covered.

Make the spring rolls: Place a wrapper in a flat dish, with one corner facing you. Place 2 tablespoons of filling in a line across this corner. Dip your fingers in the beaten egg and wet the edges of the wrapper. Fold over the corner tip holding the filling and continue to roll, folding in the sides as you do. Keep rubbing the edges with beaten egg to ensure that the roll will be sealed. The roll will be a small, finger-like cylinder. Repeat until all the rolls are made.

Deep-fry the spring rolls: Heat a wok over high heat, add 5 cups peanut oil, and heat to 350° F. Deep-fry the rolls, 4 to a batch, until golden brown, 3 to 4 minutes. Keep turning the rolls to ensure even color. Turn off the heat. Remove from the oil with a strainer and drain on paper towels.

MAKES 16 SPRING ROLLS

NOTE: Spring rolls can be frozen after cooking. To reheat, either deep-fry lightly (325° F for a minute) or heat in a 375° F oven for 3 minutes per side, until hot and crisp.

Chicken in the Wok,
Every Which Way

Cooking in a wok—stir-frying in particular—is perhaps the most enjoyable aspect of the Chinese kitchen. It is surely the most theatrical when performed by chefs with giant woks. Watching ingredients glisten, often change color, and come together as they are whisked quickly through cooking oil is very satisfying as well. There is nothing that cannot be cooked in a wok, the all-purpose concave cook pot of China and the only pot used by millions of Chinese for thousands of years.

I like to think that each time you cook in a wok it is a small journey into a culinary ritual. When foods are cooked in China the concept of balance is followed not consciously but instinctively. Tastes, textures, and aromas must be complementary. The Chinese believe that traditionally, all meals must contain a *fan,* a cooked starch, usually rice, but noodles or breads as well; *choy,* or vegetables; and *yuk,* a generic word for all nonvegetables, ranging from poultry to meats to seafood, which are wedded to *fan,* or accompany it. It is a practice followed to this day. It is a concept so ingrained in the minds of Chinese cooks that it becomes second nature. What is crucial in achieving this balance and, of course, in proper cooking, is how foods are prepared. All foods, particularly when they are to be cooked in a wok, must be prepared and cut to specific lengths, for their size dictates their cooking time. This applies to the chicken and its accompaniments in this book. Equally important is the concept that foods must be added to the wok in a prescribed order so that they will cook harmoniously.

Hard carrots, asparagus, and stalks of vegetables such as broccoli, cauliflower, and bok choy require more cooking time than do somewhat softer vegetables such as bell peppers, onions, leeks, and celery, and these in turn require more cooking time than do leaves of lettuce, spinach, and bok choy. What this means is that in stir-frying, foods must be added to the wok at different times and in order, not thrown together as one sees often in television cooking demonstrations.

Different foods react differently to the intense heat of the wok, which affects the cooking time. Some foods, as you will see, benefit from oil-blanching, water-blanching, or stock-blanching before going into a wok stir-fry.

The key to wok cooking is intense heat generated in the concave bowl of the wok, with foods being whisked quickly through small amounts of oil in the wok, a concept the Chinese call *wok hei*, or "wok air." Proper fire and proper stirring to the precise point of flavor release: that is *wok hei*. With this goes the even rhythm of the arm and hand holding the spatula, a rhythm that you will acquire quite easily, usually with your first stir-fry. Logically, foods must be thoroughly dry before going into the wok not only to avoid splatter but to prevent any residual moisture from altering cooking times.

With the dishes you will cook from this book you will discover and frequently use what I like to call the Chinese culinary trinity of ginger, garlic, and scallions. Virtually every preparation will have at least one, many two, or all three of these ingredients. They provide the base for most dishes, by preparing cooking oil to receive chicken and other vegetables and by flavoring. They are indispensable, and they, too, must be cut to specific sizes and added to oil at specific times to perform at their best.

The final key to a successful stir-fry is the moisture in the ingredients. Vegetables should be dry before cooking. If they are too wet, they will not cook properly and if they are too dry, they will not cook properly. A balance has to be maintained. Occasionally a vegetable will lose its moisture as it cooks. Always have at hand a small bowl of water when you cook with the wok so if this loss of moisture occurs, you can dip your hand into the bowl of water and splash a bit of water into the wok. This will create instant steam, will moisten the vegetables, and will cook them immediately.

All of these techniques are quickly learned, so that by your second or third stir-fry you will be cooking with ease and enjoyment, as well as with a sense of accomplishment.

Though its major function is to be used in stir-frying, the versatility of the wok and its shape allows it to be used to deep-fry, pan-fry, braise, and steam.

*T*he two preparations that follow illustrate perfectly the principle of the stir-fry. All ingredients, sauces, and marinades are prepared in advance so that the actual cooking is done quickly. The stir-fry is simple when executed properly and when ingredients are added in the order specified. I like to offer these two recipes because of the different cooking processes they entail. Another intriguing aspect is that the dishes, though they use identical marinades and sauces, taste different, simply because of the juxtaposition of their ingredients. This is surely an indication of the perfect stir-fry, which never masks the essential flavors of the food it contains. No two stir-fried dishes taste the same, or as my elders would often say to me, "ling ling, cha cha, du dum sai," which translates as "an orchestra without both a bell and a cymbal would have no variation."

Chicken Stir-Fried with Broccoli

(YUK FAR CHAU GAI PIN)

This has become a favorite dish in Chinese restaurants where, unfortunately it often has an overly thick starchy sauce and little defined taste. This is, to be sure, careless cooking. This recipe, which delineates the steps for a perfect stir-fry, is sure to please you. The broccoli needs to be water-blanched to make it tender, a process used often in stir-fries where texture is as important as taste.

FOR THE MARINADE

2 teaspoons oyster sauce

1 teaspoon light soy sauce

1 teaspoon sesame oil

2 teaspoons Shao-Hsing wine or sherry

¼ teaspoon salt

1 teaspoon sugar

Pinch white pepper

2½ teaspoons cornstarch

8 ounces chicken cutlet, cleaned thoroughly, dried, and cut into pieces 2½ inches long by 1½ inches wide by ¼ inch thick

FOR THE SAUCE

1½ tablespoons oyster sauce

1 teaspoon light soy sauce

½ teaspoon sesame oil

1½ teaspoons sugar

Pinch white pepper

1 tablespoon cornstarch

½ cup chicken stock (page 36)

FOR THE BLANCHING

1 quart boiling water

1 slice ginger, ½ inch long, lightly smashed

2 whole garlic cloves, peeled

2⅛ teaspoons salt

½ teaspoon baking soda, optional

8 ounces broccoli florets, washed, drained, and cut into pieces 2 inches long by 1½ inches wide (about 40 pieces)

2 tablespoons peanut oil

2 teaspoons minced ginger

1½ teaspoons minced garlic

1 tablespoon Shao-Hsing wine or sherry

1 tablespoon chicken stock

2 tablespoons red bell peppers cut into ¼-inch dice

Mix the marinade ingredients in a bowl. Put the chicken in the marinade, mix well, and allow to stand 20 minutes. Mix sauce ingredients in a separate bowl and reserve.

Water-blanch the broccoli. Put the boiling water and all other blanching ingredients in a pot and bring to a boil over high heat. Add the broccoli, immerse, and stir for 6 seconds, until it turns bright green. Turn off the heat. Run cold water into the pot and drain. Repeat. Allow all excess water to drain off and discard the ginger and garlic. Set the broccoli aside.

Heat a wok over high heat for 30 seconds. Add the peanut oil and coat the wok with it, using a spatula. When a wisp of white smoke appears add the ginger and garlic and stir briefly. Add the chicken and marinade and spread in a thin layer. Cook for a minute, turn the chicken over, and mix well. Add the wine by drizzling it in from the edge of the wok and mix well. If the mixture is dry, add the stock and mix well. Add the broccoli and stir-fry with the chicken for 2 minutes. Make a well in the mixture, stir the reserved sauce and pour it in. Stir to mix well until the sauce thickens and bubbles. Turn off the heat. Transfer to a preheated dish, sprinkle with the diced red peppers, and serve with cooked rice.

MAKES 4 SERVINGS

Chicken Stir-Fried with Cauliflower

(Yeh Choy Far Chau Gai Pin)

Cauliflower was virtually unknown in China until its appearance in the restaurants of Hong Kong about four decades ago, and even then it was regarded as exotic, it was called, yeh choy far, *or "flower of the cabbage." In less than twenty years it became commonplace and today is grown extensively throughout China.*

FOR THE MARINADE
   2 teaspoons oyster sauce
   1 teaspoon light soy sauce
   1 teaspoon sesame oil
   2 teaspoons Shao-Hsing wine or
      sherry
   ¼ teaspoon salt
   1 teaspoon sugar
   Pinch white pepper
   2½ teaspoons cornstarch

   8 ounces chicken cutlet, cleaned
      thoroughly, dried, and cut into
      pieces 2½ inches long by
      1½ inches wide by ¼ inch thick

FOR THE SAUCE
   1½ tablespoons oyster sauce
   1 teaspoon light soy sauce
   ½ teaspoon sesame oil
   1½ teaspoons sugar
   Pinch white pepper
   1 tablespoon cornstarch
   ½ cup chicken stock (page 36)

FOR THE BLANCHING
   1 quart boiling water
   1 slice ginger, ½ inch long, lightly
      smashed
   2 whole garlic cloves, peeled
   2⅛ teaspoons salt
   8 ounces cauliflower florets, cut into
      pieces 2 inches long by 1½ inches
      wide (about 30 pieces)
   2 ounces snow peas, ends removed,
      cut in half on the diagonal

   2 tablespoons peanut oil
   1½ teaspoons minced ginger
   1½ teaspoons minced garlic
   1 tablespoon Shao-Hsing wine or
      sherry
   ½ cup red bell pepper sliced into
      pieces 1 inch long by ½ inch wide
   2 tablespoons chicken stock

Mix the marinade ingredients in a bowl, add the chicken, and mix. Allow to rest for 20 minutes and reserve. Mix the sauce ingredients in a separate bowl and reserve.

Water-blanch the cauliflower: Put the blanching ingredients in a pot, cover, and bring to a boil over high heat. Put the cauliflower in a mesh strainer, lower it into the pot, and blanch for 2 minutes. Remove the strainer and plunge the cauliflower into ice water to stop the cooking process. Remove from the water and drain well. Reserve.

Water-blanch the snow peas: Bring the water back to a boil. Put the snow peas in the strainer and lower into the boiling water. Blanch for 20 seconds until they become bright green. Remove and run cold water over them. Drain well and reserve.

Heat a wok over high heat for 40 seconds, add the peanut oil, and coat the wok with it, using a spatula. When a wisp of white smoke appears, add the ginger and garlic and stir briefly. Add the chicken and marinade, spread them in a thin layer, and cook for a minute. Turn the mixture over, stir, and mix. Drizzle the wine along the edge of the wok and mix well. Add the cauliflower and stir-fry, mixing well. Add the snow peas and bell peppers and stir well. Add the chicken stock, stir, and cook for 2 minutes. Make a well in the mixture, stir the reserved sauce and pour it in. Mix. When the sauce thickens and bubbles, turn off the heat, transfer the mixture to a preheated dish, and serve with cooked rice.

MAKES 4 SERVINGS

Chicken Ding with Hoisin Sauce

(Gung Bo Gai Ding)

With this dish comes a bit of folklore told to me often as a child. It is said that when a gung bo, or crown prince, was traveling around China, hunger made him stop at a small restaurant, where this ding, *or dish of small square pieces, was fed to him. He is said to have interrupted his trip and returned quickly to Beijing so that he could report on this dish to the imperial cooks. Any dish called a* ding *consists of different ingredients cut into small squares, usually diced.*

FOR THE MARINADE
  ¼ teaspoon salt
  1 teaspoon sugar
  1½ teaspoons light soy sauce
  2 teaspoons Shao-Hsing wine mixed
    with 1 teaspoon ginger juice
  1½ tablespoons oyster sauce
  1 teaspoon sesame oil
  3 teaspoons cornstarch
  Pinch white pepper

12 ounces chicken cutlet, cleaned
    thoroughly, dried, and cut into
    ½-inch cubes
½ cup raw cashew nuts
3 tablespoons peanut oil

¼ teaspoon salt
1 slice ginger, ½ inch long, lightly
    smashed
½ cup string beans (ends removed)
    cut into ½-inch-long pieces
¼ cup fresh peeled and washed
    water chestnuts and cut into
    ¼-inch dice
⅓ cup bamboo shoots cut into
    ¼-inch dice
½ cup red bell pepper, cut into
    ½-inch dice
2 teaspoons minced garlic
1½ tablespoons hoisin sauce
1 tablespoon Shao-Hsing wine or
    sherry

Mix the marinade ingredients in a bowl, add the chicken, and mix well. Allow to rest for 30 minutes and reserve. Dry-roast the cashews (see page 16) until lightly browned. Reserve.

Heat a wok over high heat for 30 seconds. Add a tablespoon of the peanut oil, and coat the wok with it, using a spatula. When a wisp of white smoke appears, add the salt and ginger and stir briefly. Add the vegetables in this order: string beans, water chestnuts, bamboo shoots, and bell pepper. Stir the mixture as the ingredients are added. Cook for a minute and empty from the wok into a strainer. Drain vegetables and reserve. Wipe the wok and spatula with paper towels.

Heat the remaining 2 tablespoons of oil over high heat with the minced garlic and stir briefly. Add the hoisin sauce and mix well. Add the chicken and its marinade, spread the mixture in a thin layer, and cook for 30 seconds. Turn the mixture over. Add the wine by drizzling it in from the edge of the wok and stir well. When the chicken turns white, add the vegetables and stir-fry together for a minute. Turn off the heat. Transfer the mixture to a preheated dish, and serve with the roasted cashews.

NOTES: Cashews should be served separately, so that the diner may add them to the chicken in whatever amount they wish. If the nuts are mixed into the stir-fry they will become soggy.

The cashews may be roasted in advance. Allow to cool and keep in a covered jar. They will stay crisp for 3 days.

MAKES 4 TO 6 SERVINGS

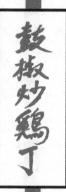

Stir-Fried Chicken
with Black Beans and Peppers

(See Jiu Chau Gai Ding)

This combination of chicken, intensely flavored fermented black beans, and bell peppers, a classic of Cantonese cooking, is another ding. *The fermented beans, particularly when mashed into a paste with fresh garlic, are a wondrous ingredient that enhances the chicken, and emits a wonderful fragrance as it is stir-fried. My daughter tells me that when coming home from school she could smell this dish cooking while still a block from our home.*

12 ounces chicken cutlet, cleaned thoroughly, dried, and cut into ¾-inch cubes

FOR THE COATING
1½ teaspoons sesame oil
½ teaspoon salt
1 teaspoon sugar
2 teaspoons cornstarch

FOR THE SAUCE
1½ tablespoons oyster sauce
½ teaspoon light soy sauce
1 teaspoon Chinese white rice wine or gin
½ teaspoon sugar
1 teaspoon sesame oil
2 teaspoons cornstarch
4 tablespoons chicken stock (page 36)
Pinch white pepper

2 tablespoons fermented black beans, rinsed and drained three times
2 large garlic cloves, peeled and smashed
3 tablespoons peanut oil
1 teaspoon minced ginger
8 ounces green bell peppers, cut into ¾-inch squares
3 tablespoons chicken stock
1 tablespoon Chinese white rice wine or gin

Put the chicken and coating ingredients in a bowl and toss to coat the chicken well. Allow the mixture to rest for 30 minutes. Mix the sauce ingredients and reserve. Mash the black beans and garlic into a paste and reserve.

Heat a wok over high heat for 30 seconds. Add a tablespoon of the peanut oil and coat the wok with it, using a spatula. When a wisp of white smoke appears, add the ginger and stir for 20 seconds. Add the bell peppers and stir and cook for

45 seconds. (The wok should be hot and dry.) Add a tablespoon of stock to moisten and create steam. The peppers are cooked at this point. Turn off the heat. Remove the peppers, and reserve.

Wipe the wok and spatula with paper towels. Reheat the wok over high heat for 20 seconds and coat with the remaining peanut oil. When a wisp of white smoke appears, add the black bean–garlic paste. Break up the paste and stir-fry for 45 seconds or until its fragrance is released. Add the chicken and coating mixture, spread it in a thin layer, and cook for 30 seconds. Turn the mixture over and mix well for a minute. Add the rice wine by drizzling it in from the edge of the wok. Stir well and mix for a minute. Add the remaining 2 tablespoons stock and stir-fry well until the chicken absorbs the liquid, 2½ to 3 minutes.

Add the peppers and mix together for a minute. Make a well in the mixture, stir the reserved sauce and pour it in. Stir and cook until the sauce is absorbed by chicken and peppers, 1 to ½ minutes. (There should be only a minimal amount of moisture in the wok at this point.) Turn off the heat. Transfer the mixture to a pre-heated dish and serve with cooked rice.

MAKES 4 TO 6 SERVINGS

Mu Shu Chicken

(Muk See Gai Yuk)

Depending upon which restaurant menu you happen to be reading, this recipe is either moo shoo, moo shi, moo shu, or mu shu, all of which are phonetic transliterations of this famous preparation from Beijing. Mu shu is best, even though these two words translate as "saw dust," to connote its many shredded ingredients. It is also known elsewhere in China as muk see, particularly in Canton and in south China, where I grew up, and that was its name for as long as I can remember. Usually prepared with pork, it is often made with chicken as well, as here.

This is a fine preparation on its own and may be eaten as is, but it is customarily eaten enclosed in pancakes.

3 cups peanut oil
8 ounces chicken cutlet, cleaned
   thoroughly, dried, and shredded

FOR THE SAUCE
1½ teaspoons Shao-Hsing wine or
   sherry
3½ teaspoons sugar
¾ teaspoon salt
2 tablespoons dark soy sauce
1 tablespoon cornstarch
2 tablespoons chicken stock
   (page 36)
2 tablespoons hoisin sauce
Pinch white pepper

1 teaspoon minced ginger
1 teaspoon minced garlic
4 cups finely shredded cabbage

3 scallions, trimmed, cut into
   1½-inch-long pieces, white parts
   quartered lengthwise
½ cup shredded bamboo shoots
2 tablespoons cloud ears, soaked in
   hot water for 30 minutes, washed
   and dried
40 tiger lily buds, soaked in hot
   water for 30 minutes, hard ends
   cut off and halved
5 dried Chinese black mushrooms,
   soaked in hot water for
   30 minutes, stems removed,
   squeezed dry, and shredded
4 eggs, lightly scrambled
1 tablespoon sesame oil
Pancakes *(bok bang)* (recipe follows)
Hoisin sauce (page 162)

Heat a wok over high heat for a minute. Add the peanut oil and heat to 350° F. Add the chicken and oil-blanch for 1½ minutes (page 16), or until the chicken turns white. Remove from the oil with a strainer and allow to drain over a bowl. Reserve. Mix the sauce ingredients in a bowl and reserve.

Empty the oil from the wok into a bowl and set aside. Return 2 tablespoons peanut oil to the wok and heat over high heat. Add the ginger and garlic and stir briefly. Add the cabbage and stir-fry for 3 minutes. Add the scallions, bamboo shoots, cloud ears, tiger lily buds, and mushrooms. Stir well and cook for another 3 minutes. Add the chicken to the mixture and stir-fry together for a minute. Make a well in the mixture, stir the reserved sauce and pour in. Mix well. When the sauce thickens, add the scrambled eggs and mix together thoroughly. Turn off the heat, add the sesame oil, and toss. The dish is now ready.

Pancakes

(Bok Bang)

There is nothing better than eating freshly made pancakes with hot mu shu chicken. Years ago, pancakes that were cooked and then frozen were important from Taiwan. All one had to do was steam them. They were highly unreliable, most often fragile and easily torn. Recently thin pancakes labeled "moo shoo wrappers" have arrived in markets. They are quite thin and elastic and I consider them adequate to use. However, they do not even approximate those you make yourself.

1¾ cups Pillsbury Best All-Purpose
  Flour, enriched, bleached, plus
  ½ cup flour for dusting

¾ cup boiling water
1½ tablespoons sesame oil

Put the flour in a mixing bowl. Slowly add the boiling water and stir in one direction with a wooden spoon. When the flour absorbs the water and cools, knead the dough into a ball and then place it on a work surface dusted with flour. Knead for about 2 minutes, until the dough is thoroughly smooth. Place in a bowl, cover with plastic wrap, and allow to rest for 30 minutes.

On a flour-dusted work surface roll the dough into a 12-inch sausage and divide into twelve 1-inch pieces. Flatten each piece with your palm, using more flour to dust if the dough is sticky. While working, cover the dough not in use with plastic wrap. Working with two pieces of dough at a time, wipe one side of each piece gently with sesame oil and place one flattened, oiled piece atop another. Roll them together into 7-inch rounds. The result is a two-layer pancake. Repeat until 6 two-layer pancakes are made.

(continued)

Heat a wok over low to medium heat for a minute. Place a double pancake in the dry wok and cook for a minute, until it begins to bubble up. (The heat in the dry wok must be carefully controlled. If it is too high, the pancakes will burn.) Turn the pancake over and cook until a few brown spots appear. Remove from the wok and separate into two layers. You will have 2 pancakes, each browned lightly on one side and white on the other. Repeat until all the dough is used and you have 12 pancakes.

Before serving, steam the pancakes in a stack for 5 to 7 minutes, until soft and hot.

To serve, place about 3 tablespoons of mu shu chicken filling in the center of the pancake, overlap the sides, and fold up the bottom to create an envelope closed on three sides but open at the top. Serve immediately.

MAKES 12 PANCAKES (4 TO 6 SERVINGS)

NOTES: These pancakes can be made ahead of time, if desired, and steamed before serving. They will keep, refrigerated, for 5 days and may be frozen for up to 3 months. Allow to defrost before steaming. The pancake recipe can be doubled or even tripled, if you wish.

These pancakes can also be eaten with Cantonese fried chicken, also known as Peking chicken (page 53). Slice the chicken meat and skin together into pieces 1 by 2 inches. Brush the pancake with hoisin sauce, place the chicken slice in the pancake, add the white parts of 6 scallions shredded into 2-inch lengths or ½ cup cucumbers shredded into 2-inch julienne, fold as above, and serve.

Hoisin Sauce

⅓ cup hoisin sauce
1 tablespoon sugar
1 tablespoon sesame oil

1 tablespoon Shao-Hsing wine or
   sherry

Combine all the ingredients in a bowl and mix well.

*T*he two recipes that follow are examples of summer stir-fries from China's tropical south, where fruits of all kinds are plentiful. Cooking with fruits, melons, and sweet gourds was and is common in the south, but in Hong Kong it is an art form that uses papayas, pumpkins, pineapples, peaches, mangos, melons, apples, and apricots.

Chicken Stir-Fried with Mango

(Mong Gua Chau Gai Pin)

In China mangos are eaten sweet and soft in teahouse sweets, as green, slightly sour pickles, dried as snacks, and in stir-fries. To be stir-fried, mangos must be sweet but firm, and as they cook their sweet fragrance is released, giving this recipe its Chinese name, which translates as "fragrant mango cooked with chicken."

FOR THE MARINADE
- ½ teaspoon ginger juice mixed with 1 teaspoon Chinese white rice wine or gin
- ¼ teaspoon salt
- ½ teaspoon sugar
- ½ teaspoon sesame oil
- 3 teaspoons oyster sauce
- 1 teaspoon light soy sauce
- 1 teaspoon cornstarch
- Pinch white pepper

- 8 ounces chicken cutlet, cleaned thoroughly, dried, and cut into slices 2 inches long by ½ inch wide by ¼ inch thick
- 2½ tablespoons scallion oil (page 38)

- 2 teaspoons minced ginger
- ½ cup mango, peeled and sliced into pieces 1 inch long by ½ inch wide by ¼ inch thick
- ½ cup scallions cut into ½-inch-long pieces on the diagonal (white parts only)
- ⅔ cup green bell peppers cut into pieces ½ inch wide, then diagonally into ½-inch lengths
- ¼ cup fresh peeled and washed water chestnuts cut into ⅛-inch-wide slices
- 1 teaspoon minced garlic
- ¼ teaspoon salt
- 2 teaspoons cornstarch mixed with ⅓ cup chicken stock (page 36)

Mix the marinade ingredients in a bowl, add the chicken, and toss. Allow the mixture to rest for 30 minutes.

Heat a wok over high heat for 40 seconds. Add a tablespoon of the scallion oil and coat the wok with it, using a spatula. When a wisp of white smoke appears, add the ginger and stir and cook for 30 seconds. Add the mango, scallions, bell pepper, and water chestnuts and stir-fry for a minute or until the peppers turn bright green. Turn off the heat, remove the vegetables from the wok, and set aside. Wipe the wok and spatula with paper towels.

Heat the wok over high heat for 20 seconds, add the remaining oil, and coat the wok with it. When a wisp of white smoke appears, add the garlic and salt. When the garlic turns light brown, add the chicken and marinade and spread the mixture in a thin layer in the bottom of the wok. Cook for a minute, turn the mixture over, and cook for another minute until the chicken turns white. Add the mango and vegetables and stir-fry for 1½ minutes. Make a well in the mixture, stir the cornstarch-stock mixture and pour it in. Cover and mix thoroughly and cook for 1½ minutes more or until the mixture thickens. Transfer to a preheated dish and serve immediately with cooked rice.

MAKES 4 SERVINGS

Chicken Stir-Fried with Honey Melon

(Mut Gua Chau Gai Pin)

This recipe from Hong Kong contains both honeydew and cantaloupe melons, which are commonly called by the same name in China, mut gua, *literally "honey melon." For the dish to be at its best, the melons should be ripe and sweet but firm. Use the flesh of the melon closest to the seeds; it's usually sweeter.*

FOR THE MARINADE
- 2 teaspoons oyster sauce
- 1½ teaspoons Shao-Hsing wine or sherry
- 1 teaspoon light soy sauce
- 1 teaspoon sesame oil
- ¾ teaspoon grated ginger
- 2 teaspoons cornstarch
- ¾ teaspoon sugar
- ½ teaspoon salt
- Pinch white pepper

8 ounces chicken cutlet, cleaned thoroughly, dried, and cut thinly across the grain, on the diagonal, into slices 2 inches wide by ¼ inch thick

- 3 tablespoons peanut oil
- ¼ teaspoon salt
- ½ cup snow peas (ends and strings removed) with each pod cut into 3 pieces on the diagonal
- 4 scallions, white parts cut into ½-inch-long pieces
- ½ honeydew melon, cut into 1-inch square slices, ¼ inch thick (about 1¼ cups)
- ½ cantaloupe, cut into 1-inch square slices, ¼ inch thick (about 1¼ cups)
- 1 tablespoon minced garlic

Mix the marinade ingredients in a bowl, add the chicken and toss. Allow the mixture to rest for 30 minutes. Reserve.

Heat a wok over high heat for 30 seconds, add a tablespoon of the peanut oil, and coat the wok with it, using a spatula. When a wisp of white smoke appears, add the salt and stir briefly. Add the snow peas and scallions and stir-fry until the snow peas turn bright green, about a minute. Add the honeydew and cantaloupe and stir-fry until just hot, about a minute. Turn off the heat. Remove the contents from the wok and set aside. Wipe the wok and spatula with paper towels.

Reheat the wok over high heat for 20 seconds. Add the remaining 2 tablespoons peanut oil and coat the wok with it. When a wisp of white smoke appears, add the garlic and stir for 30 seconds. Add the chicken and marinade, spread the mixture in a thin layer, and cook for a minute. Turn the mixture over, stir, and mix until the chicken turns white, about another minute. Add the reserved melons and vegetables and stir-fry until well-mixed and very hot, about another minute. Turn off the heat. Transfer the mixture to a preheated dish and serve immediately with cooked rice.

MAKES 4 SERVINGS

Sichuan Hot Bean Curd with Chicken

(Mah Paw Dau Fu)

The English name for this Sichuan classic does not do it justice. Traditionally it is composed of bean curd and ground pork in a hot chili–flavored sauce, but that description is inadequate as well. It is best to ask for it in restaurants by its Chinese name, for it is a dish of folklore. It is said that an elderly woman, a mah paw *notable for her pockmarked face, opened a restaurant in Sichuan and created this dish. She and the dish became so famous that people would travel great distances just to eat it, but it had no name. So it became* mah paw dau fu, *or the "pockmarked grandmother's bean curd," and it is known by that name to this day. I have adapted this traditional dish, modernized it, and replaced the pork with chicken, but it is cooked in the traditional manner.*

4 ounces chicken cutlet, cleaned
    thoroughly, dried, and ground
1 teaspoon sesame oil
Pinch salt

FOR THE SAUCE
1½ teaspoons double dark soy sauce
1½ tablespoons oyster sauce
5 tablespoons ketchup
1 tablespoon Chinkiang vinegar or
    balsamic vinegar
2 teaspoons sugar
¾ teaspoon salt
1 tablespoon Sichuan peppercorn
    paste (page 30)
1 tablespoon Shao-Hsing wine or
    sherry
1 teaspoon sesame oil

4 tablespoons chicken stock
    (page 36)
1 tablespoon cornstarch

2 tablespoons peanut oil
3 fresh Thai chilies, minced, with
    seeds
1 teaspoon minced garlic
1½ teaspoons minced ginger
4 cakes fresh firm bean curd
    (1 pound), cut into ½-inch cubes
3 to 4 scallions, white parts only, cut
    into ¼-inch pieces on the
    diagonal (¼ cup), plus ½ cup
    green parts of scallions cut into
    ¼-inch-long pieces on the
    diagonal

Mix the chicken with the sesame oil and salt. Toss to mix well and allow to rest for 20 minutes. Mix the sauce ingredients in a bowl and reserve.

    Heat a wok over high heat for 30 seconds. Add the peanut oil and coat the wok with it, using a spatula. When a wisp of white smoke appears, add the chilies, garlic, and ginger and stir for 30 seconds. Add chicken and break it up with a spatula. Add the white parts of the scallions, stir, and mix for 45 seconds. Add the bean curd and stir-fry together for 3 minutes until mixture is hot. Make a well in the mixture, stir the reserved sauce and pour it in. Stir until the sauce thickens and bubbles. Add the green parts of the scallions and mix well. Turn off the heat. Transfer the mixture to a preheated dish and serve immediately with cooked rice.

MAKES 4 SERVINGS

NOTES: This dish may be served either with cooked rice, as noted, or with cooked thin Chinese egg noodles (similar to cappellini). If you prefer the noodles, cook 8 ounces noodles in boiling water for about 3 minutes or until al dente. Drain well, place on a serving platter, and top with *mah paw dau fu*.

Bean curd comes in different textures, from soft to firm. Make your selection according to personal preference. I prefer firm, for its texture complements the other ingredients in this dish. There is no difference in the taste of soft and firm bean curd.

Chicken Stir-Fried
with Bean Sprouts and Chives

(SUB CHOY CHAU GAI SEE)

The Chinese consider this a "cooling" dish, one that lowers body heat and provides balance. Bean sprouts are cooling, as is chicken, with the critical balance supplied by the "warming" chives. The Chinese name for chives is gau choy, *or "nine vegetable," to which is added another vegetable, the bean sprouts, making the dish* sub choy, *or "ten vegetable," a Chinese play on words by its creator, Chan Wing, a master chef of Canton.*

2 quarts water
1 slice ginger, ½ inch long, lightly smashed
12 ounces mung bean sprouts, washed thoroughly to remove thin bean skins and drained well

FOR THE SAUCE
1 teaspoon light soy sauce
1½ tablespoons oyster sauce
2 teaspoons Shao-Hsing wine or sherry
1 teaspoon sesame oil
¼ teaspoon salt
1¼ teaspoons sugar
1½ tablespoons cornstarch

⅓ cup chicken stock (page 36)
Pinch white pepper

1½ tablespoons onion oil (page 39)
2 teaspoons minced ginger
2 teaspoons minced garlic
4 ounces garlic chives, washed, dried, green leaves cut into 1½-inch-long pieces, harder ends cut into ¼-inch-long pieces, reserved separately
6 ounces chicken cutlet, cleaned thoroughly, dried, and cut into 2-inch-long julienne
1 tablespoon Shao-Hsing wine or sherry

Water-blanch the bean sprouts: Put the water and ginger in a pot and bring to a boil over high heat. Add the bean sprouts and blanch for 8 seconds. Run cold water into the pot and drain well. Reserve. Mix the sauce ingredients in a bowl and reserve.

Heat a wok over high heat for 30 seconds. Add the onion oil and coat the wok with it, using a spatula. When a wisp of white smoke appears, add the minced ginger and garlic and stir briefly. Add the hard ends of the chives and stir for 30 seconds. Add the chicken, spread it in a thin layer, and cook for a minute. Turn the mixture over, mix, and cook for another 30 seconds. Drizzle the wine into the wok from the edges and mix well.

Make a well in the mixture, stir the reserved sauce and pour it in. Mix well. When the sauce thickens and bubbles, add the chive leaves, and stir. Add reserved bean sprouts, stir and mix well. Turn off the heat. Transfer to a preheated dish and serve immediately with cooked rice.

MAKES 4 SERVINGS

*T*he two recipes that follow have their roots in China's western province of Sichuan. Much, perhaps too much, is made of the heat of the foods of Sichuan, and though it is true that Sichuan's table does make liberal use of chilies and hot oils, it is also true that these hot ingredients, in the hands of fine cooks, are used judiciously for flavoring and for balance, not simply to sear the palate.

Shanghai Strange Taste Chicken

(Guai Mei Gai)

The term "strange taste" is used in Sichuan, where this description is usually applied to the regional paste of Sichuan peppercorns, ginger, and scallions. However, "strange taste" is used elsewhere and has different meanings in other parts of China, as well as different ingredients. Usually what is meant by the word strange is "unusual." So it is with this fine dish from Shanghai, the creation of master chef Lin Man Wen of the Green Villa Restaurant. It does not have the "strange taste" of sichuan peppercorn paste, yet Chef Lin acknowledges that the inspiration for this chicken recipe lies in Sichuan. I had this dish on a visit to Shanghai and I re-created it here. What is unusual about the dish is not only its intense sauce but the fact that the chicken is first cooked and then marinated, a reverse of the usual cooking procedure.

FOR THE POACHING

3 cups cold water
2 scallions, cut into thirds
1 slice ginger, 1/2 inch long, lightly
   smashed
1 1/4 teaspoons salt
2 teaspoons sugar

1 pound chicken cutlets, cleaned
   thoroughly and dried
3/4 cup cashew nuts, dry-roasted
   (page 16)
2 1/2 cups shredded iceberg lettuce

FOR THE SAUCE

3 tablespoons sesame paste, mashed
2 1/2 tablespoons light soy sauce
1 1/2 tablespoons sugar
2 teaspoons hot pepper oil
   (page 40)
1/2 teaspoon crushed Sichuan
   peppercorns
1 tablespoon minced ginger
1 tablespoon minced garlic
Pinch salt

2 tablespoons peanut oil
3/4 cup white parts of scallions cut
   into 1/4-inch-long pieces on the
   diagonal

Poach the chicken: Put the poaching ingredients in a pot, cover, and bring to a boil over high heat. Add the chicken, lower the heat to a simmer, and poach for 15 minutes. Halfway through the cooking, turn the chicken over. Turn off the heat and allow the chicken to rest in the liquid for 10 minutes.

(continued)

While the chicken poaches, dry-roast the cashew nuts and reserve. Make a bed of shredded lettuce on a serving platter and set aside. Mix the sauce ingredients and reserve.

Remove the chicken from the pot and cut it into 1-inch squares, $\frac{1}{3}$ inch thick. Put the chicken pieces in a bowl, add the sauce, and mix well to coat.

Heat a wok over high heat for 30 seconds. Add the peanut oil and coat the wok with it, using a spatula. When a wisp of white smoke appears, add the scallions and stir-fry for 20 seconds. Add the chicken and sauce, stir and mix well, and cook for a minute until the liquid evaporates and the chicken is well coated. Turn off the heat, mound the chicken on the bed of lettuce, sprinkle with roasted cashews, and serve.

MAKES 4 TO 6 SERVINGS

Old Skin Chicken

(Chun Pei Gai)

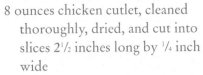

The "old skin" referred to in this Sichuan recipe is dried tangerine skin. The peels are dried in the sun then kept in sealed jars in a cool, dry place. The older the skin, the more expensive it is; some tangerine skins are ten years old. Often, tangerine skins are found in herbalist's shops, but they are readily available in Chinese and Asian groceries. Traditionally, this recipe for chicken with "old skin" was served at feasts and banquets and even at the dinners of nobles.

8 ounces chicken cutlet, cleaned thoroughly, dried, and cut into slices 2½ inches long by ¼ inch wide

1 tablespoon egg white, beaten

2 teaspoons tapioca starch

FOR THE SAUCE

1 tablespoon double dark soy sauce

3½ teaspoons sugar

⅛ teaspoon salt

1 teaspoon sesame oil

2 tablespoons Shao-Hsing wine or sherry

½ teaspoon hot pepper oil (page 40)

2 teaspoons Chinese white rice vinegar or distilled vinegar

2 tablespoons peanut oil

3 dried whole chilies

1 tablespoon Sichuan peppercorn paste (page 30)

1 teaspoon dried tangerine peel, soaked in hot water for 20 minutes until softened and cut into ½-inch-long shreds

2 teaspoons minced ginger

4 tablespoons scallions, trimmed and cut into ¼-inch-long pieces

1 tablespoon Shao-Hsing wine or sherry

Put the chicken in a bowl, add the egg white and tapioca starch and toss well to coat. Reserve. Mix the sauce ingredients in a separate bowl and reserve.

Heat a wok over high heat for 30 seconds. Add the peanut oil and coat the wok with it, using a spatula. When a wisp of white smoke appears, add the chilies, stir, and cook for 30 seconds. Add the coated chicken and spread it in a thin layer in the wok. Cook for a minute. Turn the mixture over and cook for 30 seconds more, stirring. Add the Sichuan peppercorn paste and tangerine skin and stir-fry well to mix. Add the ginger and scallions and stir and mix well. Drizzle the wine into the wok along the edges and mix well. Make a well in the mixture, stir the reserved sauce and pour it in. Cook for 2 to 3 minutes until the sauce is almost absorbed. There should be a small amount of liquid remaining. Turn off the heat. Transfer to a preheated dish and serve with cooked rice.

MAKES 4 SERVINGS

Stir-Fried Chicken with Snow Peas

(Seut Dau Gai Pin)

The lovely vegetable snow peas, which complements so many other foods yet is delicious by itself simply stir-fried with ginger, is referred to in China as hoh lan dau, *or "Holland peas," which recognizes its lineage.*

12 ounces chicken cutlets, cleaned thoroughly, dried, and sliced against the grain into 2-inch-long by 1-inch-wide pieces

1½ cups plus 2 tablespoons chicken stock (page 36)

1 slice ginger, ½ inch long, lightly smashed

FOR THE SAUCE

2 teaspoons light soy sauce

2½ tablespoons oyster sauce

2 teaspoons Shao-Hsing wine or sherry

1 teaspoon sesame oil

1½ teaspoons sugar

¼ teaspoon salt

1 tablespoon tapioca starch

Pinch white pepper

⅓ cup chicken stock

1½ tablespoons peanut oil

1½ teaspoons minced ginger

2 teaspoons minced garlic

½ teaspoon salt

8 ounce snow peas, ends and strings removed, each pod cut into thirds on the diagonal

4 scallions, trimmed, cut into ½-inch-long pieces on the diagonal, white parts lightly smashed

5 fresh water chestnuts, peeled and thinly sliced

1 tablespoon Shao-Hsing wine or sherry

Stock-blanch the chicken: Bring the 1½ cups of chicken stock and the ginger to a boil over high heat. Add the chicken and blanch until it turns white, about 1½ minutes. Turn off the heat. Remove the chicken and reserve. Mix sauce ingredients in a separate bowl and reserve.

Heat a wok over high heat for 30 seconds. Add the peanut oil and coat the wok with it, using a spatula. When a wisp of white smoke appears, add the ginger, garlic, and salt and stir briefly. Add the snow peas, scallions, and water chestnuts and stir-fry together for 45 seconds. Add the chicken and stir-fry for 30 seconds. Drizzle the wine down the edge of the wok and mix well. Add the remaining 2 tablespoons chicken stock, mix well, and cook for a minute.

(continued)

Make a well in the mixture, stir the reserved sauce and pour it in. Stir the mixture thoroughly. When the sauce begins to thicken and bubble, turn off the heat. Transfer the mixture to a preheated dish. Serve immediately with cooked rice.

Makes 4 to 6 servings

Sliced Chicken with Fresh Mushrooms

(Sin Gu Gai Pin)

This delicate preparation exists throughout China, differing only from region to region in the use of different mushrooms—black, white, brown, mottled, small, and large. However, the dish must always be made with fresh chicken and mushrooms, which is the literal translation of its Chinese name. I have made this dish with a number of mushrooms, but for this recipe I have chosen fresh, meaty porcini, the textures of which complement the chicken so well.

FOR THE MARINADE
1 tablespoon grated ginger
1½ teaspoons sesame oil
1 teaspoon Chinese white rice wine
   or gin
½ teaspoon sugar
¼ teaspoon salt
1½ teaspoons oyster sauce
½ teaspoon light soy sauce
1 teaspoon cornstarch
Pinch white pepper

8 ounces chicken cutlet, cleaned
   thoroughly, dried, and cut into
   slices 2 inches long by 1½ inches
   wide

FOR THE SAUCE
1 tablespoon oyster sauce
½ teaspoon sugar
1 teaspoon light soy sauce
½ teaspoon sesame oil

2 teaspoons cornstarch
Pinch white pepper
5 tablespoons chicken stock
   (page 36)

3½ tablespoons peanut oil
1 tablespoon minced ginger
½ teaspoon salt
6 ounces fresh porcini, stems and
   gills removed, cut into 2 by
   ¼-inch-wide julienne
6 ounces snow peas, ends and
   strings removed, cut into pieces
   1 inch long by 1½ inches wide
¼ cup bamboo shoots cut into
   pieces 1 inch long by 1½ inches
   wide
4 fresh water chestnuts, peeled and
   cut into ¼-inch-wide slices
1 tablespoon minced garlic
1 tablespoon Chinese white rice
   wine or gin

Put the marinade ingredients in a bowl, add the chicken, and mix. Allow the mixture to rest for 30 minutes. Reserve. Combine the sauce ingredients in a separate bowl and reserve.

(continued)

Heat a wok over high heat for 30 seconds, add 2 tablespoons of the peanut oil and coat the wok with it, using a spatula. When a wisp of white smoke appears, add the ginger and salt and stir briefly. Add the mushrooms and stir for 10 seconds. Add the snow peas, bamboo shoots, and water chestnuts and stir-fry for 2 minutes. Turn off the heat, transfer the contents of the wok to a bowl, and reserve. Wipe the wok and spatula with paper towels.

Reheat the wok over high heat for 20 seconds. Add the remaining 1½ tablespoons peanut oil and coat the wok with it. When a wisp of white smoke appears, add the garlic and stir briefly. When it begins to brown, add the chicken and marinade. Spread in a thin layer, and cook for a minute. Turn the chicken over, stir, and cook for another minute. Drizzle the wine into the wok from the edge, stir, and cook until the chicken is cooked through, about another minute. Add the reserved vegetables, stir, and mix for 2 minutes. Make a well in the center of the mixture, stir the reserved sauce and pour it in. Stir well and mix until the sauce thickens and bubbles, about 30 seconds. Turn off the heat. Transfer the mixture to a preheated dish. Serve with cooked rice.

MAKES 4 TO 6 SERVINGS

*T*he two recipes that follow are typical of Beijing. Much of its cooking was and is influenced by the presence of the imperial palace and its traditions. The dowager empress, China's penultimate royal ruler, loved sweet foods and much of Beijing's traditional food is indeed sweet. Beijing cooks occasionally like the heat conveyed by chilies and hot oils and prefer assertive vegetables such as onions and leeks. Chicken is a staple throughout the region, the ubiquitous Peking duck notwithstanding. In Beijing foods are often coated with eggs, starches, and batters and are oil-blanched before being stir-fried.

Chicken with Leeks, Beijing Style

(GAI TIU CHAU SUN YUK)

This preparation is what is called lao Beijing, *or "old Beijing," to indicate a dish with tradition. Leeks are eaten quite often in Beijing and in the nearby northern Shandong region, usually in combination with mutton or chicken. Their flavor complements that of chicken quite well, and the combination has a fetching sweetness to it.* Sun yuk, *part of the name for this dish, refers to the tender, crisp inside stalks of the leek. This chicken dish is eaten in Beijing, along with Steamed Lotus Leaf Breads (page 136).*

12 ounces chicken cutlet, cleaned
   thoroughly, dried, and cut into
   pieces 3 inches long by ⅓ inch
   wide (preferably meat from a
   large, thick-breasted bird, such as
   an oven roaster, usually about
   6 pounds)

FOR THE COATING
   1½ tablespoons egg white, beaten
   2 teaspoons cornstarch
   ¼ teaspoon salt
   ½ teaspoon sugar
   Pinch white pepper

FOR THE SAUCE
   1 tablespoon hoisin sauce
   ½ tablespoon double dark
      soy sauce
   1½ tablespoons Shao-Hsing wine or
      sherry

1 teaspoon Chinese white vinegar or
   distilled vinegar
1 teaspoon sugar
1½ teaspoons hot pepper oil
   (page 40)
1½ teaspoons cornstarch
3 tablespoons chicken stock (page 36)

2½ cups peanut oil
4 ounces leeks, washed well to
   remove grit, tough outer green
   portions of stalks removed, tender,
   white inner stems dried
   thoroughly and cut into
   ½-inch-wide pieces on the
   diagonal, tightly packed to yield
   1 cup
2 teaspoons minced ginger
2 teaspoons minced garlic
1 tablespoon Shao-Hsing wine or
   sherry

In a bowl, mix the chicken strips with the coating ingredients. Toss to coat well and allow to rest for 30 minutes. Mix the sauce ingredients and reserve.

Oil-blanch the chicken: Heat a wok over high heat for 45 seconds. Add the peanut oil and heat to 325° F. Add the coated chicken and turn off the heat immediately. Loosen the chicken and blanch for 1 to 1½ minutes until it is completely white. Remove from the wok with a strainer and allow to drain over a bowl.

Turn the heat back to high and heat the oil to 350° F. Add the leeks and cook for a minute until soft and wilted. Turn off the heat and remove the leeks to the strainer with the chicken.

Empty all the oil from the wok except a tablespoon. Heat the oil over high heat for 20 seconds. Add the ginger and garlic and stir briefly. Add the chicken and stir and cook for a minute. Add the wine by drizzling it in from the edge of the wok, mix well, and cook for another minute. Make a well in the mixture, stir the reserved sauce and pour it in. Stir well and cook for another minute until the sauce thickens and becomes dark brown. Add the leeks, turn off the heat, and stir well. Transfer the mixture to a preheated dish and serve with steamed lotus leaf bread or cooked rice.

MAKES 4 SERVINGS

NOTES: I suggest that you keep the outer leek leaves. Well cleaned, they will flavor a fine soup or become a good ingredient for a stock.

Strips of chicken cut 3 inches long by ⅓ inch wide are called *tiu*, or thick strips.

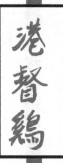

Viceroy's Chicken

(Guang Duk Gai)

This is still a classic dish in Beijing, served often at dinners in the diplomatic guest house where foreign envoys are housed. Why the preparation is named guang duk, *which translates as "viceroy" or "governor," is unclear, but in Beijing you will be told that it is an honored name. This is a dish that is supposed to indicate respect for those to whom it is served, in short, a diplomatic dish.*

Serve with Steamed Lotus Leaf Breads (page 136).

It is preferred that the meat for this dish come from a large, thick-breasted bird, such as an oven roaster, which is usually about 6 pounds.

1 pound chicken cutlet, cleaned
   thoroughly, dried, and cut into
   irregular pieces, about 1½ inches
   long by ¾ inch wide

FOR THE COATING
  2 tablespoons egg white, beaten
  ¾ teaspoon salt
  1½ teaspoons sugar
  2 tablespoons tapioca starch

FOR THE SAUCE
  1 tablespoon Chinkiang vinegar or
   balsamic vinegar
  1½ teaspoons light soy sauce
  1½ teaspoons sugar

¼ teaspoon salt
1 tablespoon Shao-Hsing wine or
  sherry
5 tablespoons ketchup
2 teaspoons hot pepper oil
  (page 40)

5 cups peanut oil
2 teaspoons minced ginger
4 dried chilies
1 small red bell pepper (8 ounces),
  cut into pieces 1½ inches long by
  ¾ inch wide, tightly packed to
  yield 1 cup
1 tablespoon Shao-Hsing wine

Put the chicken in a bowl with the coating ingredients and mix well to coat. Allow to rest for 20 minutes. Mix the sauce ingredients in a separate bowl and reserve.

Heat a wok over high heat for a minute. Add the peanut oil and heat to 325° F. Turn off the heat, add the coated chicken and separate the pieces. Turn the heat back on to medium and stir the chicken, making certain the pieces do not stick together. Cook for 1½ minutes until the chicken turns white and plump. Turn off the heat, remove the chicken with a strainer, and drain over a bowl. Empty the wok of oil.

Return a tablespoon of oil to the wok and turn the heat to high for 30 seconds. Add the ginger and chilies and stir briefly. Add the peppers and stir together briefly. Add the chicken and stir-fry together for 2 minutes. Add the wine by drizzling it in from the edge of the wok to create steam. Make a well in the mixture, stir the reserved sauce and pour it in. Stir and mix well for 2 minutes until the chicken pieces are well coated and there is no residual liquid in the wok. Turn off the heat. Transfer the mixture to a preheated dish and serve with steamed lotus leaf breads.

MAKES 4 TO 6 SERVINGS

Sweet and Sour Chicken

(Seun Tim Gai Yuk)

The concept of sweet and sour has existed in Chinese cooking for centuries, usually as a complementary and versatile sauce for chicken, fish, shrimp, and pork. The peak of its fame, however, was reached in the 1950s at a Hong Kong banquet honoring Great Britain's Prince Philip, duke of Edinburgh, when a dish of sweet and sour pork was served. It received a great deal of attention, and soon sweet and sour chicken was on the menu of most restaurants in Hong Kong. In the West, people absolutely adore sweet and sour sauces. Unfortunately, most often such sauces tend to be thick and viscous, overly sweet, and badly blended. A perfect sweet and sour sauce should be silky and balanced, not gummy.

FOR THE BATTER

- 1 cup cornstarch
- 1 cup flour, Pillsbury Best All-Purpose, preferably enriched, bleached
- ½ teaspoon salt
- 2½ tablespoons baking powder
- 12 ounces cold water
- 2 tablespoons peanut oil

FOR THE SAUCE

- ¾ cup sugar
- ½ cup tomato sauce
- ¾ cup red wine vinegar
- 1 tablespoon dark soy sauce
- 1 cup cold water
- 3 tablespoons cornstarch mixed with 3 tablespoons cold water

- 6 cups peanut oil
- 1 pound chicken cutlets, cleaned thoroughly, dried, and cut into 1-inch cubes
- 2 tablespoons cornstarch, for dusting
- ⅓ cup green bell pepper cut into ¾-inch squares
- ½ cup red bell pepper cut into ¾-inch squares
- 1 small carrot, cut into ¼-inch-wide diagonal slices
- ⅓ cup fresh pineapple (very sweet) cut into ¾-inch cubes (if unavailable, use canned, sweetened pineapple)

Mix the batter: Combine the cornstarch, flour, salt, and baking powder in a bowl. Pour in the cold water gradually, stirring clockwise with a chopstick until smooth. Add the peanut oil and blend well. Reserve. Mix the sauce ingredients, except the cornstarch-water mixture, in a small pot. Put the cornstarch-water mixture in a separate bowl and mix well. Reserve both mixtures.

Heat a wok over high heat for a minute. Add the peanut oil and heat to 350° F. While the oil heats, coat the chicken pieces with 2 tablespoons of cornstarch. Put the chicken, in batches of 6 pieces, into the batter, coating them completely. With tongs, place the coated chicken pieces, one at a time, in hot oil. Fry in two to three batches. Fry the pieces for 30 seconds, continuing to turn so that the chicken browns evenly, about 3 minutes. Remove the chicken with a strainer and drain over a bowl. Continue frying until all the chicken pieces are fried. Drain and place all pieces on a preheated platter. Reserve.

Bring all the sauce ingredients, except the cornstarch-water mixture, to a boil over medium heat. Stir the cornstarch-water mixture and pour it into the sauce pot slowly with one hand while stirring with the other until well blended. Allow the mixture to return to a boil. Add all the vegetables to the sauce, making certain they are completely immersed. Allow the mixture to return to a boil and stir. Cook for a minute and turn off the heat.

By this point all the chicken should be cooked and drained. Put the sauce in a sauce boat. Serve chicken and sauce separately by placing the chicken on a plate and pouring the sauce with the vegetables on top in the amount desired. Serve with cooked rice.

MAKES 4 TO 6 SERVINGS

NOTE: You may pour the sauce over the chicken on the platter and serve. But if there is any chicken left over, it will become soggy.

*T*he two recipes that follow are from Hunan, in the west of China, a landlocked region that preserves much of its food. Its cooking is characterized by intense, assertive flavors and is famed for its liberal use of chilies and garlic. The Chinese often refer to Hunan's food as being ideal winter eating because of the heat it generates. Hunan is also recognized for the quality of its chilies, said to be China's best and most fiery. In fact, the Chinese say that those tiny, intensely hot chilies for which Thailand is famous had their antecedents in Hunan.

Twice-Fried String Beans with Minced Chicken

(GAI YUNG CHAU SEI GUAI DAU)

This classic and spicy preparation is said to have been born in Hunan, though Sichuan claims it as well. No matter. In Hunan it is prepared with "long beans," basically string beans that grow from 18 to 24 inches in length. These long beans, thin and tender, are usually available in Asian markets, but if unavailable common string beans work nicely as well. The intensity of the heat in this dish is a personal choice, dictated by the amount of hot pepper flakes you choose to add.

4 ounces chicken cutlet, cleaned
    thoroughly, dried, and ground
1 teaspoon sesame oil
1/4 teaspoon salt

FOR THE SAUCE
2 teaspoons double dark soy sauce
1 1/2 teaspoons sugar
1/2 teaspoon salt
1 teaspoon sesame oil
1 1/2 teaspoons Chinkiang vinegar or
    balsamic vinegar
2 teaspoons Shao-Hsing wine or
    sherry

1 1/4 teaspoons hot pepper flakes
1 tablespoon cornstarch
1/3 cup chicken stock (page 36)
Pinch white pepper

5 cups peanut oil
1 pound fresh whole string beans,
    ends removed, washed, dried
    thoroughly
2 teaspoons minced ginger
2 teaspoons minced garlic
1 tablespoon Shao-Hsing wine or
    sherry

Mix the chicken well with the sesame oil and salt. Allow to rest for 20 minutes, and reserve. Mix the sauce ingredients thoroughly and reserve.

Heat a wok over high heat for a minute. Add the peanut oil and heat to 350° F. Place the string beans in a Chinese strainer and lower them into the oil. Fry for 2 1/2 minutes and turn off the heat. Remove the beans with the strainer and drain them over a bowl. (The string beans will have a shriveled look, which is the desired appearance for this dish.) Drain the oil from the wok.

Return 2 tablespoons of oil to the wok and turn the heat to high. Add the ginger and garlic and stir briefly. Add the chicken and loosen it with the spatula. Stir and mix and cook for 1 1/2 minutes or until the chicken turns white. Add the string beans and stir-fry for another 1 1/2 minutes. Add the wine by drizzling it in from the edge of the wok. Stir the mixture for 30 seconds. Make a well in the mixture, stir the reserved sauce and pour it in. Stir and mix well and cook until the sauce thickens. (The string beans should be thoroughly coated and there should be no residual liquid in the wok.) Turn off the heat and transfer the mixture to a pre-heated dish. Serve with cooked rice or with steamed lotus leaf breads (page 136).

MAKES 4 TO 6 SERVINGS

Hunan Pepper Chicken

(HUNAN LOT GAI)

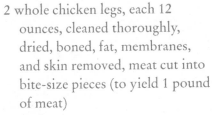

This traditional recipe from Hunan uses the chicken leg meat. It is believed by some in Hunan that the darker meat is more flavorful and more moist than breast meat. This dish also makes use of chilies and of Sichuan peppercorns, which the Hunanese seem to like as much as their neighbors in Sichuan.

2 whole chicken legs, each 12 ounces, cleaned thoroughly, dried, boned, fat, membranes, and skin removed, meat cut into bite-size pieces (to yield 1 pound of meat)

1 egg, beaten

¼ teaspoon salt

¼ teaspoon crushed Sichuan peppercorns

2 tablespoons cornstarch

FOR THE SAUCE

2 tablespoons dark soy sauce

1½ teaspoons minced garlic

2 teaspoons minced ginger

1½ tablespoons hoisin sauce

1 tablespoons sugar

1 tablespoon Chinkiang vinegar or balsamic vinegar

2 teaspoons Shao-Hsing wine or sherry

4 cups peanut oil

¼ cup scallions cut into ⅛-inch-wide julienne (white parts only)

8 to 10 small dried hot chili peppers

Mix the chicken pieces with beaten egg, salt, peppercorns, and 1 tablespoon of the cornstarch. Allow to marinate for 5 minutes and reserve. Mix the sauce ingredients in a separate bowl and reserve.

Heat a wok over high heat for 40 seconds, add the peanut oil, and heat to 350° F. Sprinkle the remaining tablespoon of cornstarch over the chicken pieces. Place in a Chinese strainer and lower into hot oil. Deep-fry for 3 to 4 minutes, turning to ensure the pieces brown evenly, until they are crisp. Turn off the heat, remove the pieces with a strainer, and drain over a bowl.

Empty the wok of oil and place it back over the heat. When the oil residue is hot, add the scallions and chili peppers and stir for about 40 seconds. Add the chicken pieces and stir-fry until well mixed. Stir the reserved sauce and pour it into the wok. Stir-fry all the ingredients until the chicken pieces are thoroughly coated with sauce, about 3 minutes. (There should be no liquid remaining in the wok.) Turn off the heat and transfer the mixture to a preheated dish. Serve with cooked rice.

MAKES 4 TO 6 SERVINGS

Eight-Piece Chicken

(Jah Bat Fai)

炸八塊

This is a classic banquet dish from Fujian and one that connotes great good luck. Its name translates as "fried eight pieces." The number eight in Chinese mythology represents the Eight Immortals in Heaven, and the number eight recurs throughout China in many aspects of life. One sees the number eight in sequence in artistic decorations and on license plates. People open new businesses on the eighth day of a month, engagements and weddings are scheduled for eighth days, and the eighth day of the eighth month is very special indeed. In Fujian this dish is usually made with a small chicken cut into eight pieces—the legs in half and the two halves of the breast in half for a total of eight pieces. My adaptation uses a large and meaty breast; otherwise, the dish is cooked as it is in Fujian.

This dish is excellent served with Steamed Lotus Leaf Breads (page 136).

It is preferred that the chicken cutlets be cut from a large breast of a large bird, such as an oven roaster, usually about 6 pounds.

1 pound chicken cutlets, cleaned thoroughly, dried, and cut into 8 thick pieces, each about 3 inches long by 1½ inches wide by 1½ inches thick

FOR THE MARINADE
1 tablespoon Shao-Hsing wine or sherry
1 tablespoon finely sliced scallions
1 teaspoon minced ginger
1 teaspoon sugar
¼ teaspoon salt

FOR THE DIPPING SAUCE
1 tablespoon Chinkiang vinegar or balsamic vinegar
1 tablespoon light soy sauce
2 teaspoons sugar
1 tablespoon Shao-Hsing wine or sherry

8 cups peanut oil
⅓ cup tapioca starch
1½ tablespoons finely sliced scallions

Put the chicken and marinade ingredients in a bowl and mix well. Allow to rest for 20 minutes and reserve. Mix the sauce ingredients in a separate bowl and reserve.

Heat a wok over high heat for a minute. Add the oil and heat it to 350° F. While the oil heats, dredge each piece of chicken in tapioca starch until well coated.

(continued)

Shake off excess starch. Place all 8 pieces in a Chinese strainer and lower them into the oil. Deep-fry the chicken with a strainer in the wok, turning constantly until the chicken becomes golden brown, about 5 minutes. Turn off the heat. Remove the chicken, strain over a bowl, and transfer to a preheated dish. Sprinkle the chicken with scallions, and serve with the reserved dipping sauce.

MAKES 4 SERVINGS

*T*he four recipes that follow constitute a family. All are based upon my basic minced chicken filling recipe. Three of them use my recipe as a filling or stuffing. Filling foods or stuffing them with other foods is a tradition in China, the filling being usually minced fish or shrimp. I have modified this custom by using minced chicken to great advantage, for chicken changes the tastes of these traditional preparations for the better. The other change I have made is in the cooking technique.

Ordinarily these filled and stuffed restaurant dishes would be cooked in very large woks over low Chinese stoves, so that the foods to be fried could be spread out and cook evenly. For the home kitchen I have found that a cast-iron or nonstick skillet gives the best result.

The fourth recipe in this small family is a variation of a much loved preparation from Shanghai, in which my filling recipe is used on its own, without stuffing, to create a large chicken meatball which is then pan-fried. Here as well I have altered tradition by making the recipe with minced chicken rather than the traditional pork. As my father always told me, you must learn to turn corners or make adaptations, for if you only follow one path you will walk into a wall.

Asparagus Wrapped in Minced Chicken

(Gai Yeong Bau Lo Sun)

For this wrapping, my minced chicken recipe replaces minced carp, a popular fresh-water fish beloved in Hangzhou and one that is quite often used for fillings. The change to minced chicken is for the better, with its firmer texture and more defined taste.

1 recipe basic minced chicken filling (page 41)	8 asparagus spears, cut into 5-inch lengths as measured from the tips
4 cups cold water	1 teaspoon salt
½ teaspoon baking soda, optional	3 tablespoons peanut oil

Prepare the basic minced chicken filling and reserve.

In a large pot bring the water, baking soda, and salt to a boil over high heat. Water-blanch the asparagus. Add the spears to the boiling water and blanch until they turn bright green, about 30 seconds. Drain, refresh under cold water, and allow to dry on paper towels. (The recipe can be prepared in advance to this point. Cover and refrigerate the minced chicken and the blanched asparagus.)

When the filling cools, divide it into 8 equal portions. With your palm, flatten each portion into a 3-inch-long oval wide enough to enclose the base of an asparagus spear. Press the base into the oval and fold the chicken to enclose the spear firmly. You will have what I call an asparagus lollipop, with the tip of the spear protruding.

Heat a cast-iron skillet over high heat for 45 seconds (or a nonstick pan for 10 seconds). Add 2 tablespoons or more, if needed, of the peanut oil, just enough to cover the bottom of the pan. When a wisp of white smoke appears, place the wrapped asparagus in the skillet and lower the heat to medium. Fry until golden brown, about 1½ minutes on each of the four sides of each wrapped spear. Remove the asparagus to paper towels to drain. Turn off the heat. When all are fried and drained, place on a preheated platter and serve immediately.

MAKES 4 SERVINGS

NOTE: To reheat leftover wrapped asparagus, allow to return to room temperature and then pan-fry over medium heat for 5 to 6 minutes until hot.

Eggplant Stuffed with Minced Chicken

(Yeung Ai Gua)

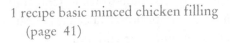

Eggplant is a versatile vegetable in China, enjoyed steamed, stir-fried, deep-fried, and braised. It is often stuffed, a popular method particularly in the dim sum kitchen, where its stuffing is usually minced shrimp, carp, or other white fish. By stuffing eggplant with minced chicken, perhaps I have begun a new tradition.

1 recipe basic minced chicken filling
   (page 41)

FOR THE SAUCE
   3 tablespoons oyster sauce
   2 teaspoons double dark soy sauce
   1 teaspoon light soy sauce
   1 tablespoon Chinese white rice
      wine or gin
   1 tablespoon sesame oil

3½ teaspoons sugar
Pinch white pepper
2½ tablespoons cornstarch
1½ cups chicken stock (page 36)

2 Chinese eggplants, each about
   10 inches long
1 tablespoon cornstarch
4 tablespoons peanut oil

Prepare the basic minced chicken filling and reserve. Mix the sauce ingredients in a small bowl and reserve.

Cut off the ends of the eggplant on the diagonal and discard. Cut the eggplant, still on the diagonal, at ¼-inch intervals, the first cut halfway through the eggplant to form a pocket and the second cut all the way through to create a slice. Continue until there are 16 such slices with pockets. (I have included extra eggplant with this recipe so that you can perfect, with practice, your cutting.)

Divide the minced chicken into 16 equal portions. Dust the inside of each eggplant pocket with cornstarch and then with a butter knife pack each pocket with portion of filling, allowing a ridge to protrude. Repeat until there are 16 stuffed slices.

Heat a cast-iron skillet over high heat for 30 seconds (or a nonstick pan for 8 seconds) and put 2 tablespoons of the peanut oil in the skillet. When a wisp of white smoke appears, put 8 eggplant slices in the oil, stuffed sides down. Lower the heat to medium and fry for 2½ minutes until golden brown. Turn the eggplant over to a flat side, fry 2 minutes more, and repeat with the other flat side. Remove the eggplant and reserve. Turn the heat back to high, add the remaining 2 table-spoons oil, and repeat the process with remaining 8 slices. Turn off the heat.

Stir the reserved sauce and pour it into the frying pan. Turn the heat to medium and cook, stirring continually, until the sauce thickens and bubbles. Put the eggplant slices back into the skillet and coat them well with sauce. Turn off the heat. Transfer the mixture to a preheated dish. Serve immediately.

MAKES 16 SLICES TO SERVE 4 AS A MAIN DISH, 8 AS AN APPETIZER

NOTE: To reheat leftover stuffed eggplant, allow to come to room temperature and pan-fry over medium heat for 6 minutes, or until hot. You can also heat the eggplant in the oven at in a 325° F for 10 to 15 minutes, or until hot.

Bean Curd Stuffed with Minced Chicken

(GAI YUNG YEONG DAU FU)

For this dish I prefer to use fresh, firm bean curd. Every effort should be made to obtain fresh bean curd, which will keep stored in the refrigerator in a container of fresh water. It will stay fresh for ten days if the water is changed daily. This recipe is based upon a homestyle recipe of both the Hakka and Chiu Chow people, who customarily stuff bean curd with minced shrimp. I have changed the filling to minced chicken.

1 recipe basic minced chicken filling (page 41)	1 tablespoon cornstarch
8 cakes fresh, firm bean curd	4 tablespoons peanut oil

Prepare the basic minced chicken filling. Divide the mixture into 16 equal portions and reserve.

Allow the bean curd to drain well through a large Chinese strainer for about an hour. Pat dry with paper towels. Cut each cake in half diagonally and, with a sharp-pointed knife, cut out a pocket in each half. Dust the pocket with cornstarch and fill each with a portion of minced chicken filling. Pack the mixture in smoothly with a knife or your fingers.

Heat a cast-iron skillet over high heat for 45 seconds (10 seconds if using a nonstick pan). Add 2 tablespoons of the oil to the pan. When a wisp of white smoke appears, add 8 stuffed bean curd halves, stuffed sides down. Lower the heat to medium and fry for 3 minutes. Turn the cakes over and fry each side for 3 minutes. Remove the bean curd to a preheated serving dish. Add the remaining 2 tablespoons oil to the skillet and repeat the process with the 8 remaining bean curd halves. Remove to a heated dish, turn off the heat, and serve immediately with Sichuan peppercorn salt (recipe follows).

MAKES 16 HALVES TO SERVE 8

NOTES: This recipe may be halved, to yield 4 servings, if desired.

Stuffed bean curd leftovers may be reheated. Allow to come to room temperature and then pan-fry over medium heat for 10 minutes or until hot. Or heat the bean curd in the oven at 325° F for 10 to 15 minutes or until heated through.

(continued)

Sichuan Peppercorn Salt

1 teaspoon Sichuan peppercorns, finely ground
1 tablespoon salt

Heat a wok over high heat for 20 seconds. Add the peppercorns and stir and dry-roast (see page 16) for about a minute until they release their fragrance. Reduce the heat to low. Add the salt, stir and mix well with the peppercorns, and roast for another 2 minutes. Turn off the heat. Place the mixture in a small dish and serve with stuffed bean curd halves. (The seasoned salt may be prepared in advance and kept in a tightly sealed jar.)

Lion's Heads

(See Ji Tau)

A tradition in Shanghai for centuries, as well as in nearby Yangzhou, this preparation is distinguished by its unusual appearance: large, slightly flattened balls of meat sauced and served with small stalk vegetables known as Shanghai bok choy. The meatballs are called "lion's heads" simply because of their size. Usually the balls are made of ground pork and pork fat, browned, and then cooked together with the bok choy in a clay pot or casserole; or they are cooked alone and then served with the bok choy and covered with a thick sauce. As far as I have been able to determine they have never been made with any meat except pork, until now. I have made my own lion's heads with my basic minced chicken filling recipe with great success.

These are especially good with Steamed Lotus Leaf Breads (page 136).

Double recipe basic minced chicken
    filling (page 41)

FOR THE SAUCE
1½ tablespoons cornstarch mixed
    with 1½ tablespoons water
4 teaspoons double dark soy sauce
2 teaspoons sugar
2 tablespoons oyster sauce

3 tablespoons peanut oil
1½ cups chicken stock (page 36)
4 bulbs Shanghai bok choy
    (1 pound), each quartered, green
    leaves trimmed to a point,
    washed and dried

FOR THE BLANCHING
2 quarts water
1 tablespoon salt
¾ teaspoon baking soda, optional

Make the minced chicken filling and refrigerate covered for 4 hours or overnight, uncovered, before use. Mix the sauce ingredients in a separate bowl and reserve.

Make the lion's heads meatballs: Coat your hands with peanut oil and rub a large dish that will hold the lion's heads lightly with peanut oil. Divide the minced chicken filling recipe into 4 equal parts and form into 4 large round chicken meatballs, pressing them slightly to flatten them a bit. (They will look like fat hamburgers.) After forming the first, moisten your hands again with peanut oil. Repeat until all 4 balls are made; place in the oiled dish.

Heat a cast-iron skillet over high heat for 45 seconds (10 seconds for a nonstick pan) and add the peanut oil. When a wisp of white smoke appears, add the meat-balls. Reduce the heat to medium and fry on one side for 2 minutes until browned. Turn the balls over and repeat. Add the chicken stock to the skillet, turn the heat back to high, and bring to a boil. Lower the heat to medium and cover the skillet, leaving a small opening at the edge. Simmer the meatballs for $3\frac{1}{2}$ minutes, turn over, and cook for another $3\frac{1}{2}$ minutes. Reserve the lion's heads in a preheated dish.

While the lion's heads simmer, water-blanch the bok choy: In a pot, bring the water, salt, and baking soda to a boil over high heat. Add the bok choy and blanch for 3 minutes or until tender.

To serve, drain the bok choy and place it around the edges of a preheated plat-ter as a border. Place the lion's heads in the center of the platter. Turn the heat back to high, stir the reserved sauce and pour it in. Stir in one direction until the sauce thickens and bubbles. Turn off the heat and pour the sauce over the lion's heads. Serve immediately.

MAKES 4 SERVINGS

NOTE: To reheat the lion's heads, allow to come to room temperature. Place in a skillet over low heat with the sauce, cover, and cook for 10 minutes or until hot. If there is no sauce left, or the meatballs are dry, add 2 to 3 tablespoons of chicken stock to the skillet, just enough to cook the balls without soupiness.

Chicken Roasted with Onions and Soy Sauce

(See Chung Siu Gai)

This tried and true recipe, a Hong Kong tradition of chicken roasted in the Chinese manner, has a long history in my family. It is the dish I have made when, because of circumstances, our family has not eaten together: my older son off to swimming practice, my daughter to ballet, and my younger son to lacrosse. Or I am off to a cooking class and I must leave dinner in the oven.

3 pounds chicken breasts, with bones and skin, cleaned thoroughly but with some of its fat retained, and dried; each breast cut into quarters

2 tablespoons Chinese white rice wine or gin

3 tablespoons double dark soy sauce

1 tablespoon sesame oil

1½ teaspoons salt

1½ tablespoons sugar

1 tablespoon Chinese white rice vinegar or distilled vinegar

1 teaspoon fresh ground black pepper

4 garlic cloves, thinly sliced

1½ tablespoons peanut oil

4 cups thinly sliced onions

Place the chicken pieces in a roasting pan and toss with the rice wine or gin, soy sauce, sesame oil, salt, sugar, rice vinegar, and pepper. Put the garlic slices on and under the chicken pieces. Allow to rest for 30 minutes. Preheat the oven to 375° F.

Heat a wok over high heat for 30 seconds, add the peanut oil, and coat the wok with it, using a spatula. When a wisp of white smoke appears, add the onions. Stir and cook for a minute, lower the heat to medium, and cook for another 3 minutes until onions are soft. Turn off the heat.

Spoon the onions over, around, and under the chicken pieces. Place the roasting pan with the chicken and onions in the preheated oven and roast for 30 minutes. Lower the heat to 350° F, turn the chicken over, and roast for another 30 minutes. Turn the chicken over again and cook for a final 30 minutes, basting halfway through. Turn off the heat. Transfer the chicken to a heated platter and serve with cooked rice.

MAKES 6 SERVINGS

NOTE: This dish will remain ready to eat for as long as 3 hours in a warm oven (about 175° F) covered with foil. A whole pot of cooked rice, covered, will stay warm in the same oven.

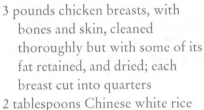

Curried Chicken

(Gah Lei Gai)

I was introduced to the taste and art of the curry when I lived in Hong Kong. The curries there were brought by immigrants from India and Pakistan, and they remain a custom to this day in that sizable community. This curry recipe is derived from one cooked by the wife of the owner of the fabric shop I managed for a time in Hong Kong. His name was Dialam Sujanani, and the curry made by his wife, who I knew only as See Tau Paw, or "Boss's Wife," was truly Indian, yet it had been slightly altered by culinary influences in Hong Kong. Often the curries there, and particularly among Chinese chefs, do not contain any coconut milk, a traditional ingredient. This is such a curry, yet it is thick and intensely flavored and cooked in a Chinese manner.

FOR THE MARINADE

2 tablespoons Chinese white rice wine or gin

1 1/2 teaspoons salt

1 1/2 tablespoons sugar

2 tablespoons cornstarch

1 teaspoon sesame oil

3 pounds chicken breasts, with bones and skin, cleaned thoroughly, but with some of the fat retained, dried, and cut into bite-size pieces

FOR THE CURRY PASTE

5 tablespoons curry powder

2 teaspoons cayenne pepper

5 1/2 tablespoons water

3 tablespoons peanut oil

1 1/2 cups onions cut into 1/4-inch dice, tightly packed

1 tablespoon minced ginger

2 teaspoons minced garlic

4 tablespoons finely sliced fresh coriander

5 chicken bouillon cubes, cut into small pieces

2 tablespoons Chinese white rice wine or gin

One 28-ounce can crushed tomatoes

Mix the marinade ingredients in a bowl, add the chicken pieces, and mix well. Allow to rest for 30 minutes and reserve. In a separate bowl, mix the curry paste ingredients until smooth and reserve.

Heat a wok over high heat for 30 seconds. Add a tablespoon of the peanut oil and coat the wok with it, using a spatula. When a wisp of white smoke appears, add the onions. Stir and cook for a minute, lower the heat to medium, and continue to stir and cook until the onions become translucent, about 2 minutes. Turn off the heat. Remove the onions to a dish and reserve.

Turn the heat back to high. Add the remaining 2 tablespoons peanut oil and coat the wok with it, using a spatula. When a wisp of white smoke appears, add the ginger, garlic, coriander, and bouillon and stir briefly. Add the curry paste and stir. Cook the mixture until the curry releases its fragrance, about a minute. Add the chicken and marinade and stir to mix well. Cook for 2 minutes until the chicken pieces are well coated. Add the rice wine and toss to mix. Add the tomatoes and their juices and stir-fry until well mixed.

Transfer the contents of wok to a nonstick pot. Bring the mixture to a boil over medium heat. Stir and mix, lower the heat, and simmer, uncovered, for an hour, stirring often with a wooden spoon. The chicken will be tender, the sauce thick and glossy. Turn off the heat. Transfer the mixture to a preheated deep dish. Serve with cooked rice.

MAKES 6 SERVINGS

NOTE: I have made this recipe for 6 servings simply because leftover curry seems to taste even better the second time around, after its many flavors combine. Reheated, this curry is quite delicious. To reheat, allow the curry to come to room temperature and place in a nonstick pot. Heat over low to medium heat until hot, 10 to 12 minutes, stirring frequently.

Concubine Chicken

(GUAI FEI GAI)

This is a fanciful dish from Sichuan. Guai Fei was said to have been an exquisitely beautiful concubine of the emperor in Chang'an, so beautiful in fact that the emperor neglected his affairs of state just so he could spend all of his time with her. How this dish of chicken wings—which is interpreted in various ways in various parts of China in tribute to Guai Fei—came to be named for her is not clear. What is clear, however, is that this dish of caramelized chicken wings from Sichuan is as attractive as it is tasty, worthy to be named for this imperial consort.

8 cups water

1 slice ginger, 1 inch long, lightly smashed

1 tablespoon salt

3 pounds chicken wings (28 to 30), washed well and drained

4 tablespoons peanut oil

3½ ounces rock sugar, crushed, or ⅓ cup plus 1 tablespoon white sugar

3 tablespoons light soy sauce, mixed with 1 tablespoon mushroom soy sauce

3 tablespoons Shao-Hsing wine or sherry

1½ tablespoons minced ginger

1½ tablespoons minced garlic

24 whole black mushrooms, 1½ inches in diameter, soaked in hot water for 30 minutes until soft, rinsed, squeezed dry of excess water, stems removed, and reserved

2 cups chicken stock (page 36)

2 teaspoons mushroom soy sauce

Put the water, ginger, and salt in a pot, cover, and bring to a boil over high heat. Add the chicken wings and water-blanch for 2½ minutes (see page 16). Turn off the heat. Run cold water into the pot to rinse and drain. Repeat. (This removes fat.) Dry thoroughly with paper towels. Reserve.

Heat a wok over high heat for 30 seconds. Add the peanut oil and bring to a boil. (White smoke will appear.) Add the sugar, lower the heat to medium, and cook, stirring, until the sugar liquefies and becomes brown and glistening but not burned, about 3 minutes. (Always control the heat to prevent burning.)

Add the reserved chicken wings and turn the heat back to high. Stir and mix to coat the wings, about 1½ minutes. Add the soy sauce mixture, stir, and mix well. Add the wine and mix well. Add the ginger and garlic and mix well. Lower the heat to medium and continue to stir until the chicken is well coated and glazed, about 7 minutes. (About $\frac{1}{3}$ cup of liquid will remain and will be quite like a syrup.) Turn off the heat.

Transfer the contents of the wok to a nonstick pot. Add the mushrooms and $1\frac{1}{4}$ cups of the chicken stock and mix well. Cover and bring to a boil over high heat. Add the mushroom soy sauce and stir and mix well. Lower the heat and cover, leaving the lid open a crack. Simmer for 1 hour and 15 minutes or until the wings are tender and almost falling off the bone. Stir and turn the wings over during cooking to prevent sticking. If the liquid dries up, you may have to add stock; if so, add $\frac{1}{4}$ cup at a time. (Do not add too much stock.) The liquid should be thick and rich; about $\frac{1}{2}$ cup should remain in the pot. Turn off the heat. Transfer the wings to a preheated platter and serve.

MAKES 28 TO 30 WINGS

NOTES: The sauce and mushrooms are perfect with cooked rice. I recommend them as a side dish to the concubine chicken.

Individual finger bowls are a must when serving concubine chicken.

Concubine Chicken II

(Guai Fei Gai Yee Ho)

This is a modern version of this Sichuan classic. I have named it for Guai Fei, but I add yee ho or "number two," to its name to indicate that it is my personal homage to her chicken. This adaptation is designed for the Western palate, which seems to love chicken wings in all guises. I am not entirely certain whether the emperor or his concubine would like my version, but I think that they surely would.

8 cups water
1 slice ginger, 1 inch long, lightly smashed
1 tablespoon salt
3 pounds chicken wings (28 to 30), washed well and dried
4 tablespoons peanut oil
3 ounces rock sugar, crushed, or 1/3 cup plus 1 tablespoon white sugar

3 tablespoons light soy sauce mixed with 1 tablespoon mushroom soy sauce
3 tablespoons Shao-Hsing wine or sherry
1 tablespoon minced ginger
1 tablespoon minced garlic

Put the water, ginger, and salt in a pot and bring to a boil over high heat. Add the chicken wings and water-blanch for 2½ minutes (see page 16). (This removes much of the fat.) Turn off the heat. Run water into the pot to rinse and drain. Repeat. Dry the wings thoroughly with paper towels and reserve.

Preheat the oven to 400° F. Line a cookie sheet with foil and set aside.

Heat a wok over high heat for 30 seconds. Add the peanut oil and bring to a boil. (White smoke will appear.) Add the sugar and stir, lower the heat to medium, and cook, stirring, until the sugar liquefies and becomes brown and glistening but not burned, about 3 minutes. (Always control the heat to prevent burning.) Add the chicken wings to the wok and turn the heat back to high. Stir and mix to coat the wings, about 1½ minutes. Add the soy sauce mixture and mix well. Add the wine and mix well. Add the ginger and garlic and mix well. Lower the heat to medium and continue to stir until the chicken is well coated and glazed, about 7 minutes. (About 1/3 cup of liquid will remain and will be quite like a syrup.) Turn off the heat.

Transfer the contents of the wok to the foil-lined cookie sheet. Place the cookie sheet in the oven and roast for 30 minutes total: 15 minutes at 400° F and 15 minutes at 450° F. The wings should be turned twice while roasting. If the liquid in the cookie sheet dries out, add 2 to 3 tablespoons water to moisten. (The wings will be browned with a caramelized gloss.) Turn off the heat. Transfer the wings to a preheated platter. Serve.

MAKES 28 TO 30 WINGS

NOTE: Individual finger bowls are a must when serving both versions of concubine chicken.

*T*he two recipes that follow are based on the same basic ingredients, chicken and fermented black beans. They illustrate perfectly the versatility and adaptability of Chinese cooking. Various cooking techniques are used—deep-frying, stir-frying, braising, and steaming—to arrive at two very different dishes. The first is a traditional restaurant preparation, the second one for the home. The first uses an entire chicken, cut up; the second, chicken cutlets. The result of the first is a dish of intensity and richness; the second, one of delicate flavors and lightness.

Braised Chicken in Black Bean Sauce

(Dau See Mun Gai)

This traditional dish, so fragrant with fermented black beans and garlic, is interpreted by just about every chef in Hong Kong. There is not one master chef who does not fancy himself the best at preparing it, for the temptation of chicken with those beans and garlic is irresistible. The aroma alone is sufficient to draw you in from the sidewalk. This dish is very special as well because it uses three major cooking techniques. It is a lesson on a plate.

FOR THE PASTE

6 whole garlic cloves, peeled
5 tablespoons fermented black beans, washed several times to remove excess salt and drained well

FOR THE SAUCE

3 tablespoons oyster sauce
1½ teaspoons sugar
½ teaspoons salt
1 tablespoon dark soy sauce

One 3½-pound chicken, cleaned thoroughly, dried, cut into bite-size pieces (page 19)
3½ tablespoons cornstarch
6 cups plus 2 tablespoons peanut oil
3 tablespoons Chinese white rice wine or gin
1 cup chicken stock (page 36)
10 sprigs fresh coriander for garnish

Mash the paste ingredients until smooth and reserve. Mix the sauce ingredients in a separate bowl and reserve.

Coat the chicken pieces with the cornstarch. Heat a wok over high heat, add the 6 cups peanut oil, and heat to 375° F. Deep-fry the chicken pieces by lowering them into the oil with a Chinese strainer. Fry for 1½ minutes or until the red blush is gone from the skin. Remove the chicken, drain, and reserve. Drain the oil from the wok and wipe it dry.

Heat the wok over high heat for 20 seconds, add the remaining 2 tablespoons peanut oil, and coat the wok with it, using a spatula. When a wisp of white smoke appears, add the garlic–black bean paste and break it up with a spatula. When the garlic is browned, add the chicken pieces and stir-fry well to mix. Add the wine by drizzling it in from the edge of the wok and mix briefly. Stir the reserved sauce and add to the wok. Mix until the chicken pieces are well coated. Turn off the heat. *(continued)*

Transfer the chicken to a nonstick pot. Pour ¾ cup of the chicken stock into the wok to help collect residual juices and then pour it into the pot over the chicken. Cover the pot and cook over low heat until the chicken is tender, 30 to 40 minutes, stirring every 10 minutes. If sauce thickens too much add a little stock, 1 to 2 tablespoons at a time. Turn off the heat. Transfer the chicken and sauce to a preheated platter. Garnish with coriander sprigs and serve with cooked rice.

MAKES 6 SERVINGS

Chicken Steamed with Black Beans

(Dau See Jing Gai)

This is my adaptation of a traditional home-cooked dish. Its style differs completely from that of the previous dish. Here, I steam boneless chicken breasts with my Sichuan peppercorn paste to provide a more delicate flavor than that of the robust tastes of the previous recipe. In these days of the overuse and casual use of words in regard to food, I say with some caution that this recipe is a "light" version of the previous recipe: similar tastes in differing degrees.

1½ pounds chicken cutlets, cleaned thoroughly, dried, and cut into 1-inch cubes

2 tablespoons tapioca starch

3 tablespoons fermented black beans, washed several times to remove excess salt and drained well

2 tablespoons Sichuan peppercorn paste (page 30)

1 tablespoon minced garlic

1 teaspoon ginger juice

2 tablespoons Shao-Hsing wine or sherry

2 tablespoons oyster sauce

2 teaspoons dark soy sauce

3 tablespoons scallion oil (page 38)

2 teaspoons sugar

½ teaspoon salt

Pinch white pepper

3 tablespoons finely sliced fresh coriander

Put all the ingredients except the coriander in a bowl. Toss and mix well to coat the chicken thoroughly and evenly. Put the chicken and the contents of the bowl in a steamproof dish. Place the dish in a steamer and steam for 40 minutes until the chicken cooks through. Halfway through the cooking, turn the chicken over. Turn off the heat. Remove the steamer to a platter. Sprinkle the chicken with the coriander and serve from the steamer with cooked rice.

MAKES 4 TO 6 SERVINGS

Steamed Chicken Custard

(Dau Fu Jing Gai Yung)

This is a classic dish with different antecedents. In western China, particularly in Hunan, it is customarily made with salty Yunnan ham. In eastern and southern China, it is made with chicken, often with shrimp, and occasionally with fish. What makes this dish unique, however, is that wherever it is made it has essentially the same custard-like texture, what the Chinese call lo siu ping on, *or "suitable for young and old." The custard itself is a blend of bean curd, eggs, and the chicken itself.*

6 ounces chicken cutlet, cleaned
    thoroughly, dried, and ground
2 cakes soft bean curd (8 ounces),
    mashed
3 large eggs, beaten
1 teaspoon grated ginger
1/4 cup finely sliced scallions
1 1/2 tablespoons oyster sauce
1 teaspoon light soy sauce
1 tablespoon white peppercorn oil
    (page 39)

1/2 teaspoon salt
1 1/4 teaspoons sugar
1 tablespoon tapioca starch
1/8 teaspoon white pepper
1 tablespoon Chinese white rice
    wine or gin
4 tablespoons chicken stock
    (page 36)

Combine all the ingredients in a bowl and mix well until thoroughly blended. (The mixture should reassemble a puree.) Place the mixture in a steamproof dish and place the dish in a steamer. Steam for 10 minutes until the custard sets. Turn off the heat. Remove the dish from the steamer and serve immediately with cooked rice.

MAKES 4 TO 6 SERVINGS

NOTE: Much of the success of this dish lies in its garnishes and toppings. I recommend that the custard be topped with 3 tablespoons of cooked fresh green peas or 3 tablespoons of finely sliced fresh coriander. Garnish according to your taste.

Chicken Steamed with Fresh Lemons

(SAI LING MUNG CHING GAI)

In China, sai ling mung *means "foreign lemon," and this dish is best made not with the thick-skinned domestic lemons from Guangzhou but with those imported from the "Golden Mountain" of California. "Foreign lemons" are deemed more fragrant. There are many versions of this combination of chicken and lemons, almost all of them called "lemon chicken," surely one of the best-known dishes on Chinese restaurant menus. In most versions, however, even in China, the chicken is coated and fried and then a thickened yellow lemon-flavored sauce is poured over it. This is not the most pleasant dish to me, for too often the sauce is too thick and viscous. I prefer to steam the chicken with fresh lemons, which results in a dish of impeccable lightness and delicacy.*

1 pound chicken cutlets, cleaned thoroughly, dried, and cut into 1-inch cubes

½ fresh lemon, squeezed to yield 1 tablespoon juice; lemon half cut into 4 pieces and reserved

¾ teaspoon ginger juice mixed with 1½ tablespoons Shao-Hsing wine or sherry

2 teaspoons light soy sauce

2 tablespoons oyster sauce

½ teaspoon salt

2½ teaspoons sugar

1 teaspoon sesame oil

1½ tablespoons peanut oil

Pinch white pepper

1½ tablespoons cornstarch

2 tablespoons red bell pepper, minced, for garnish

Put all the ingredients except the bell peppers in a bowl and toss well to mix and coat the chicken. Allow marinate and rest for 20 minutes.

Put the chicken and its marinade in a steamproof dish. Place the dish in a steamer and steam for 20 minutes or until the chicken cooks through. Halfway through the steaming process, turn the chicken over. Turn off the heat. Remove the steamproof dish from the steamer. Sprinkle the chicken with the bell peppers and serve each portion with a piece of cut lemon and cooked rice.

MAKES 4 SERVINGS

Cloud Ear Chicken

(Won Yee Jing Gai)

The Chinese translation of this preparation is "steamed cloud ears with chicken." In the garden of our house in the village of Siu Lo Chun where I grew up, there was a guava tree. It was pretty and brought sweet fruit, but what made it important to my mother, Miu Hau, was that on its base a fine crop of the flower-like cloud ear fungus grew constantly. My mother believed that the cloud ears from her guava tree were the sweetest, and she would use them and tiger lily buds gathered from our garden and dried for this dish, which she loved to cook and which we loved to eat.

1 pound chicken cutlets, cleaned thoroughly, dried, and cut across the grain into slices 2 inches long by 1/8 inch wide

3 tablespoons cloud ears, soaked in hot water for 30 minutes, rinsed 3 times and drained well

50 tiger lily buds, soaked in hot water for 30 minutes, hard ends removed, and buds halved

1 teaspoon ginger juice mixed with 2 teaspoons Shao-Hsing wine or sherry

2 tablespoons oyster sauce

1 tablespoon light soy sauce

1 1/2 tablespoons peanut oil

1 teaspoon sesame oil

1/4 teaspoon salt

1 1/2 teaspoons sugar

1 1/2 tablespoons cornstarch

2 tablespoons chicken stock (page 36)

Pinch white pepper

6 sprigs fresh coriander for garnish

Combine all the ingredients except the coriander in a bowl. Mix well to coat the chicken and allow to marinate for 20 minutes. Place the contents in a steamproof dish and place the dish in a steamer. Steam for 20 minutes until the chicken cooks through. Halfway through, turn the mixture over. Turn off the heat. Garnish with coriander and serve in the steamproof dish with cooked rice.

MAKES 4 SERVINGS

A Final Feast

MAH-JONGG CHICKEN

*T*his very special chicken feast is distinctive for its origins—mixed to be sure—and claimed by both the eastern city of Ningbo and the southern city of Guangzhou. The claim extends beyond the chicken dish itself to the game of mah-jongg, which is claimed to have been invented by both regions. The three chicken preparations that constitute the single feast, all of which are prepared from one chicken, were and are served at the end of a night of mah-jongg gaming.

Mah-jongg itself is a game of 144 tiles beautifully etched with calligraphy, numbers, and designs. It is said to be three thousand years old. Though its origins lie in southeastern China, it has become a universal game played throughout China and in much of the rest of the world as well. Its tiles are used to create sets very much as in dominoes. The illustrations, designs, and calligraphy draw upon mythology and folklore. The highest in accrued points are tiles with red and black dots and circles, referred to as Heaven, Earth, Men, and Women, sets of opposites, which set up contests. In addition, there are other sets illustrated by designs on the tiles: Bamboo, depicted by stylized bamboo stalks of different values; Honors, intricately carved scenes, the most important of which represent the north, east, south, and west winds; and calligraphic characters referred to as Dragons, the Seasons, and Flowers.

The object of this very convoluted and not easily learned game is not only to create sets and accumulate points but to create an impregnable "wall" of sets and thus high points, the winner being the person who gathers the most points. I do not play the game but I like to watch others play, and enjoy the squeals of delight that come with scoring a good tile and the groans of disappointment when a poor tile is chosen. I also enjoy the clacking of the tiles as the players smack them down on the playing table for emphasis. To this day, every restaurant of sufficient size throughout China as well as Chinese restaurants abroad have a few private mah-jongg rooms to which customers can move for an evening's amusement. Some are elaborate, offering wines, whiskies, brandies, and selections of exotic teas. Even at important family feasts such as weddings, birthdays, family reunions, and anniversaries, mah-jongg is not neglected. Invitations to such functions usually call for guests to arrive at six in the evening, three hours before the traditional dinner time of nine o'clock, to permit preliminary playing of mah-jongg. (Which is not to say that there will not be more mah-jongg at the end of the party!) And the custom of mah-jongg chicken lingers as well, always prepared by the restaurant with mah-jongg rooms.

I remember well the mah-jongg nights in Kowloon during my two years with my "number five aunt," Ng Gu Jeh, to whose house I came to live when I left Siu Lo Chun at the age of twelve. A small room behind her dry goods store was the gaming site for her mah-jongg playing friends, her small, personal "casino." Some evening there would be four players, or one table; other nights, eight players, or two tables. Always there would be friends of my aunt, in particular Dr. Chow, a Western-educated physician, who came to play mah-jongg when we were well and to treat us when we were ill, often simultaneously.

They would play for hours. No great amounts of money were won or lost during these sessions, but there was much laughter and occasional grunts of frustration that brought a good deal of teasing. I would pour cups of the strong Bo Lei tea my aunt loved as the adults played into the night. When it was late, someone would suggest that the time was right for "big chicken, three tastes," the traditional name for mah-jongg chicken, and an order was sent out to a restaurant. The evening ended with the players eating chicken and soup and rehashing the play.

My favorite cousin, Wei Sung, religiously reserved every Wednesday night as mah-jongg night, even setting aside this one night her studies to become a nurse. Other relatives were mah-jongg addicts and at their urging—because they occasionally lacked one of the four "legs" necessary to play—I tried to learn the game. It was a futile exercise. I simply was unable to grasp its niceties and was given the nickname of *dai dun op*, which simply means "big unintelligent duck." I preferred cooking.

These are fond and happy memories for me out of which I have re-created mah-jongg chicken.

Whether you prepare mah-jongg chicken traditionally or in the simplified version, you should serve it in the Chinese manner. The steamed chicken with ginger and scallions, the chicken soup with Tianjin bok choy, and the stir-fried chicken with mixed vegetables should be served simultaneously, family style, with the bowl of cooked rice in the center of the table. *"Ho ho sik,"* as the Chinese say. Good eating!

Mah-Jongg Chicken

(MAH-JONGG GAI)

Big Chicken, Three Tastes

(DAI GAI SAM MEI)

Both names for this unique and festive preparation, Mah-Jongg Chicken and Big Chicken, Three Tastes, are of equal importance. Use the one of your choice. What follows are the traditional recipes for this three-dish feast eaten after mah-jongg. To immerse yourself in the experience of preparing foods as the Chinese have done for hundreds of years, I recommend you cook with tradition. You may wish to experience this dish in a simpler way, so after each individual recipe, I have set down a simplified version. The results you will achieve using either method will be equally satisfying to be sure, but I urge you to enjoy cooking in a classic way.

Because the three chicken dishes, or "tastes," are eaten at the same time, all the ingredients, from chicken to vegetables, should be cut and ready to be cooked. The stock should be prepared and the marinades should be mixed, as should the sauce for the stir-fry. The rice should be prepared and kept warm. Then you are ready to begin. As the steamed chicken cooks, make the soup and stir-fry the chicken with vegetables. As I have stressed throughout this book, the secret to successful Chinese cooking lies in the organization of ingredients. This recipe illustrates this point quite well.

First you must prepare the stock.

Mah-Jongg Chicken Stock

One 5½-pound chicken (such as an oven roaster), cleaned thoroughly and dried

FOR THE STOCK
½ pound onions, sliced
3 whole garlic cloves, peeled

1 slice ginger, ½ inch long, lightly smashed
2 teaspoons salt
8½ cups cold water
2 tablespoons Shao-Hsing wine or sherry
1 recipe Perfect Cooked Rice (page 37)

Cut up the chicken (page 19), and bone, to yield about 1¾ pounds of leg, thigh, and wing meat. Bone the chicken breasts (page 20), to yield about 1½ pounds breast meat. Retain the giblets, neck, and bones, wing tips, leg and thigh bones, and breast bones and skin, for the stock.

Make a stock: Put all the giblets, the neck, wing tips, legs, thighs, breast, and backbones, and skin in a large pot with all the stock ingredients except the wine. Cover and bring to a boil over high heat. Immediately lower the heat and simmer, covered, leaving a small opening at the lid. After 10 minutes, residue and fat will rise to the surface; skim off and discard. Repeat in about another 10 minutes. After skimming, add the wine, stir and mix, and simmer for another 2 hours. Turn off the heat and strain the stock. Discard all bones and solids. (This should yield 6 cups of stock.) Reserve.

While the stock cooks, prepare the rice. Reserve. (Rice may be kept up to 1½ hours in a warm oven, to be eaten hot with individual chicken dishes.)

SIMPLIFIED VERSION: Instead of cutting up and boning a whole chicken, you may use 3 pounds of chicken cutlets (large, meaty breasts preferred), cleaned thoroughly and dried, cut as specified in the individual recipes. Instead of making the mah-jongg stock, you may use chicken stock (page 36). Whichever choice you make, traditional or simplified, you will need to make perfect cooked rice (page 37). Whatever your choice, you will now be ready to prepare the individual recipes that comprise the big chicken, three tastes feast.

Steamed Chicken with Ginger and Scallions

(Geung Chung Jing Gai)

2½ pounds chicken meat (all leg, thigh, and wing meat, and ¾ pound of breast meat from the boned chicken), cut into bite-size pieces

2 tablespoons shredded ginger

6 scallions, trimmed, white parts cut into 2-inch-long sections and quartered lengthwise plus 3 tablespoons finely sliced green parts scallions

1½ teaspoons ginger juice mixed with 1½ tablespoons Chinese white rice wine or gin

1¼ teaspoons salt

1½ tablespoons sugar

2 tablespoons oyster sauce

1 tablespoon Chinese white vinegar or distilled white vinegar

1½ teaspoons sesame oil

2 tablespoons peanut oil

2 tablespoons cornstarch

Pinch white pepper

Put the chicken and all other ingredients except the green parts of the scallions in a large bowl. Mix well to combine. Allow to marinate for 1½ hours.

Put the chicken and marinade ingredients in a steamproof dish or cake pan. Place the dish or pan in a steamer, cover, and steam for 45 minutes to an hour or until the chicken is tender. Every 20 minutes add boiling water to the wok to replace any water that has evaporated. Turn off the heat. Sprinkle the dish with green portions of scallions and serve from the steaming dish. Leave the steaming dish in the bamboo steamer. Serve with cooked rice.

MAKES 6 SERVINGS

SIMPLIFIED VERSION: For this recipe cut 2¼ pounds of chicken cutlets into 1¼-inch cubes. The chicken pieces should be marinated for an hour only. Steaming time will be 30 to 40 minutes. All other ingredients and cooking processes remain the same as in the traditional version.

Chicken Soup with Tianjin Bok Choy

(Jun Bak Gai Tong)

5½ cups mah-jongg chicken stock (page 221), or chicken stock (page 36)
1 slice ginger, ½ inch long, lightly smashed

1½ pounds Tianjin bok choy, leafy stalks separated and washed well, drained, stalks and leaves cut across into ½-inch-wide pieces; cut stalks and leaves separated

Put the chicken stock and the ginger in a large pot, cover, and bring to a boil over high heat. Add the Tianjin bok choy stalks, stir, and allow the stock to return to a boil. Lower the heat to medium and cook for 5 minutes, covered. Add the bok choy leaves and stir, making certain they are immersed in the stock. Cook for 3 minutes, or until tender. Turn off the heat. Cover the pot and allow the soup to remain hot until serving.

MAKES 6 SERVINGS

Stir-Fried Chicken with Mixed Vegetables

(Jup Choi Chau Gai Pin)

FOR THE MARINADE
1 tablespoon oyster sauce
½ teaspoon salt
1 teaspoon sugar
1½ teaspoons sesame oil
¾ teaspoon ginger juice mixed with
  2 teaspoons Shao-Hsing wine or
  sherry
2 teaspoons light soy sauce
2 teaspoons cornstarch
Pinch white pepper

¾ pound boned chicken breast
  meat, cut into pieces 2 inches
  long by ¼ inch wide

FOR THE SAUCE
½ teaspoon sesame oil
¼ teaspoon salt
1 teaspoon sugar
1 tablespoon oyster sauce
2 teaspoons Shao-Hsing wine or
  sherry

1 teaspoon light soy sauce
2 teaspoons cornstarch
Pinch white pepper
¼ cup chicken stock

3 tablespoons peanut oil
¼ teaspoon salt
1½ teaspoons minced ginger
6 ounces snow peas, ends and
  strings removed, cut in half on
  the diagonal
¾ cup red bell pepper cut into
  pieces 2 inches long by ¼ inch
  wide
⅓ cup fresh peeled, washed, and
  dried water chestnuts cut into
  ⅛-inch-wide slices
1½ teaspoons minced garlic
1 tablespoon Shao-Hsing wine or
  sherry

Mix the marinade ingredients in a bowl and add the chicken. Toss to coat well, allow to rest for 20 minutes and reserve. Mix the sauce ingredients in a separate bowl and reserve.

Heat a wok over high heat for 30 seconds. Add 1 tablespoon of the peanut oil and coat the wok with it, using a spatula. When a wisp of white smoke appears, add the salt and ginger and stir briefly. Add the snow peas, stir and mix well, and cook for 1½ minutes. Add the bell peppers and water chestnuts and stir-fry for 2 minutes. Turn off the heat, remove the mixture from the wok, and reserve. Wipe off the wok and spatula.

Heat the wok over high heat for 20 seconds, add the remaining 2 tablespoons peanut oil, and coat the wok with it. When a wisp of white smoke appears, add the garlic and stir briefly. Add the chicken and marinade, spread it in a thin layer, and cook for a minute. Turn over and mix well. Drizzle the wine into the wok from its edge and stir to mix well. Add the reserved vegetables, stir-fry, and cook for 2 minutes. Make a well in the mixture, stir the reserved sauce and pour it in. Stir-fry, mixing thoroughly. Cook for 2 minutes until the sauce thickens. Turn off the heat. Transfer the mixture to a preheated dish. Serve with cooked rice.

MAKES 6 SERVINGS

SIMPLIFIED VERSION: The only difference between the traditional and simplified versions is the source of the chicken meat, either from the boned breast of a whole chicken or from chicken cutlets. The stock used may be the mah-jongg stock (page 221) prepared for the traditional dish or my chicken stock (page 36). Otherwise all ingredients in the recipe are the same.

Conversions

LIQUID

Ounces	Cups	Milliliters
⅛	1 tsp	5
¼	2 tsp	10
½	1 Tbsp	14
1	2 Tbsp	28
2	¼ cup	56
4	½ cup	110
6	¾ cup	170
8	1 cup	225
10	1¼ cups	280
12	1½ cups	340
16	2 cups	450
20	2½ cups	560
24	3 cups	675
32	4 cups	900

SOLID

Ounces	Grams
1	28
2	56
3½	100
4 (¼ lb)	112
6	168
8 (½ lb)	225
9	250
12 (¾ lb)	340
16 (1 lb)	450

OVEN TEMPERATURES

Fahrenheit	Celsius	Description
225	110	Cool
275	140	
300	150	
350	180	Warm
375	190	
400	200	Warm to Hot
425	220	Hot
450	230	
475	240	Very Hot
500	250	Extremely Hot

Index

lime leaves, in Ching Ping chicken, 47
ling mung gai mein, 124
Lin Man Weu, 173
lion's heads, 201–2
Li Yu, 3
lo mein, chicken, 120–21
long beans, *see* string beans
Lo Pak Wen, 7
lot jiu yau, 40
lotus (or bamboo) leaves, 27
    breads, steamed, 136–37
    rice with chicken and, 101–2
Lunar New Year celebration, 1, 43

M

mah-jongg, 217–18
mah-jongg chicken, 217–25
    soup with Tianjin bok choy, 223
    steamed, with ginger and scallions,
       222
    stir-fried, with mixed vegetables,
       224–25
    stock, 221
mah-jongg gai, 220–25
mah paw dau fu, 168–69
mai jee gai see gun, 76
maltose, 27
mango, chicken stir-fried with, 164–65
marinades:
    for beggar's chicken, 45–46
    for chicken congee, 99
    for chicken ding with hoisin sauce,
       156–57
    for chicken stir-fried with broccoli or
       cauliflower, 152–55
    for chicken stir-fried with honey melon,
       166–67
    for chicken stir-fried with mango,
       164–65
    for corn soup with chicken, 86
    for cucumber and chicken soup, 85

    for curried chicken, 204–5
    for eight-piece chicken, 193–94
    for grated winter melon soup with
       minced chicken, 83–84
    for hot and sour soup, 81–82
    for Mou Tai chicken, 50–51, 52
    for rice noodles with chicken and black
       beans, 128
    for sliced chicken with fresh
       mushrooms, 179–80
    for spinach soup with chicken and bean
       threads, 90
    for steamed chicken buns, 131–32
    for stir-fried chicken with mixed
       vegetables, 224–25
    for tomato, potato and chicken soup,
       91–92
melon salad, chicken and, 67
minced chicken, 195
    asparagus wrapped, 196
    bean curd stuffed with, 199–200
    eggplant stuffed with, 197–98
    in lion's heads, 201–2
    twice-fried string beans with, 189–90
minced chicken filling, basic, 41, 195
minced chicken soup, 93
Ming Dynasty, 3, 91
Miu Hau, 216
mong gua chau gai pin, 164–65
Mongolia, 48
moo shu wrappers, 35
mot gua gai sah lut, 67
Mou Tai chicken, 50–51
Mou Tai chicken II, 52
muk see gai yuk, 160–62
mushrooms:
    black, in concubine chicken, 206–7
    sliced chicken with fresh, 179–80
    steamed black, 42
    see also cloud ears
mushroom soy sauce, 58
mu shu chicken, 160–62

INDEX